C000004100

# TOTALLY
# LOVEABLE

# TOTALLY LOVEABLE

A MINDFUL GUIDE TO MOVING ON
FROM TOXIC RELATIONSHIPS AND
CREATING THE LOVE YOU DESERVE

TAMMY LOVELL
*founder of* THE MINDFUL DIVA

First published in the United Kingdom by:
Independent Publishing Network

Author: Tammy Lovell
Email: info@themindfuldiva.com
Website: www.themindfuldiva.com
Please direct all enquiries to the author.

Text © Tammy Lovell, 2022
Cover and interior design: Leah Kent
The moral rights of the author have been asserted.

All rights reserved. No part of this book may be reproduced in any form, including photocopying and recording, without permission in writing from the publisher, other than for 'fair use' as brief quotations embodied in articles and reviews.

The information given in this book should not be treated as a substitute for professional medical advice. Always consult a medical practitioner. Any use of information in this book is at the reader's discretion and risk. Neither author or publisher can be held responsible for any loss, claim or damage arising out of the use, or misuse, of the suggestions made, failure to take medical advice or for any material on third party websites.

A catalogue record for this book is available from the British Library.
ISBN: 978-1-80068-708-0
E-book ISBN: 978-1-80068-709-7

*For awakening women everywhere*

# CONTENTS

# YOU ARE TOTALLY LOVEABLE

Darling, you are *Totally Loveable*.

From the crown of your head to the tips of your toes. The dark secrets of your past, the desires of your heart, the shame of things that happened in your childhood, the times when you were rejected or bullied, the abuse you suffered, the parts which society says are unacceptable or inferior, the bits of your body you think are ugly.

They are all *Totally Loveable*.

You don't have to change, you don't need to lose weight, or get more spiritual, or be more successful to be loved. You are *Totally Loveable* exactly as you are.

You probably don't believe me right now and there's a good reason for that. Everything in our society is geared towards telling you that you're not enough: from advertising that says you need to spend money to be whole, to the media full of images of women who don't look like you, even your schooling and the expectations of your family.

All these things are social conditioning.

It's not surprising you question your worthiness with so many forces against you.

Not good enough, not pretty enough, too fat, too skinny, too weird, not clever enough, too loud, too quiet, too opinionated, too old, too young, too poor, too posh, too slutty, too shy, too arrogant, too much. Society tells us we are all these things and more.

None of it is true.

You are perfect. Exactly as you are right now. You are a beautiful manifestation of the divine on Earth and you deserve to be cherished and adored.

This may sound unbelievable, but please stay with me. I'm going to take you on a journey back to your-self. Take my hand and I'll lead the way...

# INTRODUCTION

"Every block of stone has a statue inside it and
it is the task of the sculptor to discover it. I saw the
angel in the marble and carved until I set him free."
– Michelangelo

For many years, I struggled to believe I was loveable.
I found it hard to believe that I was even likeable.
Deep down I felt there was something fundamentally
wrong with me that meant I would never have the
loving relationship I craved. I was sure anyone I cared
for would eventually discover the dirty secret of my
unworthiness and abandon me.

If this sounds overly dramatic, pessimistic, or unreal-
istic then congratulations – you don't need this book.
If you relate – read on, I wrote this for you.

After splitting up with my husband of 10 years, I was completely unprepared for life as a single woman. The endless emotional roller coaster of messaging and meeting strangers; the miscommunication, the vague texts, the ghosting and confusion.

Man after man I dated would fizzle out. His ex would turn up or he'd become distant. Even when things were going well, I'd start having intense emotional triggers around what he said or did. On some deep level, I didn't believe I deserved to be happy or have what I desired without struggle and suffering. There was a wound inside me, and I didn't feel good enough for a stable relationship. It took me eight years to mend my heart and finally find love again.

When I was married, I'd been thrilled by the tales my single friends recounted of their dating lives. I lived vicariously through those stories of nights out, torrid texts, hot sex, emotional highs and lows. Secretly I feared I'd missed out. Online dating was still in its infant stage when I'd met my husband back in 2003, but now it seemed an exciting prospect. Imagine a world where you could meet an eligible bachelor with the click of a button.

Fast forward to 2013, the year my marriage fell apart and I was back on the singles' scene at the age of 36.

With the wounds from my failed relationship, I was like a bleeding animal thrown into a pool of sharks. My dating experience before marriage had consisted of meeting a guy (usually in a pub), snogging him (usually drunk) and then becoming a couple. Relationships seemed much simpler back in those days.

Now the rules were unclear. If you were texting with a man, seeing him on a regular basis, even having sex with him, it didn't mean you were a couple. New terms appeared like *friends with benefits, hook-ups, being exclusive,* and *ghosting.* All concepts I had little experience of outside my *Sex and the City* boxset. I had no idea how to negotiate this unfamiliar terrain.

The first man I dated after my marriage was like a raft to a drowning woman. I jumped from the turbulent ship of my failed relationship onto what I thought was a lifeboat. Little did I know that it would be more like the Titanic. What I really needed was to stop relying on being rescued and face those choppy emotional waters alone. It was time to sink or swim.

This book is about how I went from heartbroken, lost, and lonely to healed, happy and in love. But more than that, I want this to be a guide for you.

I'm now in the kind of relationship I always dreamt of. My partner ticks every item on my list and more. There's no better feeling in the world than feeling supported and loved by the right person.

But this book isn't just about getting into a relationship. It's about doing the inner work, so that you know and believe you are enough with or without a partner. If my man walked out on me tomorrow, I would still feel loveable because that knowing comes from inside. Romantic love is just the delicious cherry on top of self-love.

As well as manifesting a beautiful partnership, I've stepped into my soul's purpose as a mindfulness coach guiding people to transform their lives. I specialise in helping people going through hard times to recognise their worthiness and fall in love with themselves. I feel blessed every day to be of service and living my truth.

Each step of my journey unfolded in a mystical way with clues coming to me from multiple sources like a trail of clues in a treasure hunt. Only in this case, the ultimate treasure was discovering myself.

Over the last nine years, I've studied the energy and frequency of love. I've explored how to become an energetic match for love, attract it into my life and have an amazing romantic relationship.

My path included a twin flame journey, love and sex addiction recovery, healing from narcissistic abuse, full moon dancing, sugar daddy dating, practicing Tantra, learning orgasmic meditation, training as a mindfulness teacher, and eventually calling in a soulmate partner. You could say it's been a wild ride!

When you've experienced heartbreak, it can be hard to believe there's someone out there for you. If you've picked up this book, there's a good chance you're feeling sad and alone. You may feel like strategies for successful dating don't seem to work for you. You may have read every book you could get your hands on about love, relationships and sex and still feel stuck.

Maybe you've had reiki, tried counselling, started meditating, and diligently filled in your gratitude journal every day for the last six months and yet still don't feel healed. You could be starting to think that love isn't for you and your true path is to become a nun or focus solely on your career.

Maybe you're wondering *where the hell is my soulmate?*

Yep, I've been there. I've thought all these things and more. Don't worry; I've got your back. There is love, hope and healing ahead, I promise you.

They say to write the book that you once needed yourself and that's what I've done. I'm going to give you the exact steps I took to heal my heart, rediscover myself and manifest love.

Remember this is a practical guide. By completing the embodiment exercises in each chapter you'll see the best results.

I suggest that you buy a special journal to record your progress. I've created the *Totally Loveable Journal* to accompany this book, which is available from Amazon. Alternatively, there is a free printable version you can download from my website at: **www.themindfuldiva.com/book**

Intellectually knowing this information isn't enough – it's embodying it that will lead to transformation. Are you ready to do the work? OK then, let's commence.

# A NOTE ON GENDER

I've written this book from my point of view as a heterosexual female whose struggles have been very specifically with men. For ease and clarity, I will refer to the reader as she/her and the object of their affection as he/him throughout. But that's not to say this work can't be applied to anyone who wants to rediscover themselves after heartbreak.

If you're a woman who loves women, a man who loves women, a man who loves men, bisexual, non-binary, gender fluid, or any of the infinite combinations that exist then please substitute for the pronouns and genders of your choice. Love is love and the basic principles of healing your heart apply to everyone.

In this book I will also sometimes refer to feminine and masculine. These polarities do not refer exclusively to gender, but to the energies inherent in all of us. I'll discuss this further in a later chapter.

## SOULMATE RELATIONSHIPS

The term 'soulmate relationship' can have many meanings, but in the context of this book, I use it to mean a healthy, loving, stable, secure partnership which meets all your desires.

I believe that when you do the inner work this will be reflected in your external circumstances. If you have unhealed wounds, limiting beliefs and negative stories these will be mirrored back to you by the partners you choose. As you will read in this book, I attracted a 'twin flame' relationship, which triggered my deepest pain, blocks and trauma. My healing journey originally began because I wanted to get him back. What happened instead is that after I'd done my inner work, I manifested a partner who reflects the level of self-love and self-worth I've developed.

I see my current partner as a beautiful manifestation of the Universe's love for me. I used to think love had to be something dramatic, explosive, intense and painful. Now I know it gets to be simple, relaxed, nourishing and fun.

This healing journey may not always be easy – there will be painful beliefs about yourself to be examined, but this will be a process of gradually letting go of more and more baggage and revealing the beauty underneath.

It's not about changing, improving or even self-development. Like history's greatest sculptor, Michelangelo, said of creating his masterpiece *David*: "The sculpture is already complete within the marble block before I start my work. It is already there; I just have to chisel away the superfluous material."

It's time to chip away at all the pain, stories, beliefs and struggles that are in your way and reveal the truth of who you really are – a valuable being who deserves the relationship and life of their dreams.

# CHAPTER ONE

# LETTING GO WITH LOVE

"When I let go of what I am, I become what I might be."
– Lao Tzu

When my marriage ended, I found consolation in three things: booze, cigarettes, and men. At the time, my two daughters were the tender ages of two and seven. I worked three days a week as a journalist at a large healthcare organisation and had only just stopped breastfeeding my youngest.

For the previous year, my life had largely consisted of working in Central London, coming home exhausted to put the kids to bed, rinse and repeat. Life was an endless treadmill of early mornings, getting my daughters off to childcare, commuting for three hours a day on packed Tubes, making family dinners, cajoling children to sleep and, if I was lucky, watching a bit of TV before passing out and rising to do it all again.

I'm sure that in a loving household this routine could have felt much better, but my husband and I had grown irrevocably apart. There were no loving words or hugs to make life seem less harsh, no romance or even fun times at the weekend to look forward to. Our connection had died somewhere along the way, and we lived practically separate lives.

On a Friday night, he would go to the pub after work, and I would have a movie night with my daughters. We'd watch *Barbie* DVDs in our pyjamas while munching pizza and popcorn. Then, after tucking them into bed, I'd go to sleep alone.

I wished my husband would be there on those nights and for a long time I continued to invite him - imagining us ending the busy week cuddled together as a family. Sometimes he'd promise to leave the pub early to join us, but he never showed up. The lure of his social life was too appealing compared to what he saw as the monotony of domestic life. Eventually, I stopped inviting him or even hoping he would come.

On Saturdays he was too hungover to do anything together. I would suggest walks in the park, trips to museums, or visits to National Trust properties, but he would angrily tell me that I didn't know how tiring it was working full-time. He preferred to spend his weekends catching up on sleep, watching football and staring at his iPad. I felt more and more alone as the days went by. I supposedly had the dream life – a husband, career, and two kids – but it felt like I was slowly dying inside without love or affection.

When we finally decided to end our marriage, I jumped straight into a relationship with a former colleague. He was a tall, dark and intriguing man I'd chatted to at a work Christmas party once. We hadn't spoken again since. Now, years later, I found myself reconnecting with him on Facebook.

On our first date, I was as ridiculously excited as a teenage girl going to the school disco with her crush. He seemed to me the perfect man: a successful journalist and published author who was sensitive, in tune with his emotions and, most importantly, into me. It was everything I'd been missing in my marriage.

I was like a wilting flower starved of water and he was the rain. I flourished under his attention, but at the same time, I was developing a dangerous dependency. After longing for affection and attention for so long, I fell wholeheartedly for his smooth words, gentle touch and flattery.

Early on, I told him about having to move out of my marital home and fears about where I would live with my children. He replied that I could always move in with him. Those words, so carelessly uttered in the heat of the moment, were the security I longed for, and I held onto them hopefully.

Rather than face the pain of my crumbling relationship with my husband, the uncertainty of life as a single mum of two small children and the financial hardships I was going through, it was easier to focus on the drama of whether my new lover had texted me, to analyse his every word and move and spend my time planning my outfit for our next date. As far as I was concerned, he was my lifeboat and if I clung to him for dear life everything would be OK.

Dear reader, you won't be surprised to learn that he was not all he seemed. No other human is ever the answer to all our problems. This was not, as I first thought, the man sent to hand me my perfect life on a plate. Instead, he was the one sent to crack me open.

Soon it became clear that he couldn't honour the promise of offering me a place to live or indeed any promise. He became unreliable, flaky, sometimes not texting back for days or cancelling dates at the last minute on flimsy premises.

I felt abandoned, rejected and lost. I hadn't yet discovered the strength within me and had made him my higher power and reason to feel good. If I could only make things work with him, I thought everything would be all right.

But it turned out he had his own problems, pain and obsessions, which included serious mental health issues. At a time when my life was falling apart with two small children relying on me, I became his supporter and shoulder to cry on as I tried to help him through his own maze of pain. Although I hadn't learnt the term for it yet, I was totally co-dependent.

I thought love was obsession, pain, desperation, inability to sleep or eat or think of anything else. The kind of love we hear about in so many love songs and films. I was dangerously infatuated.

# TWIN FLAME JOURNEY

During this time, I became fascinated with the idea that I'd met my 'twin flame'. If you're familiar with this term, you may be aware there is a spiritual belief that originated from the ancient Greek philosopher Plato that humans were first born with four arms, four legs and two heads, but were split in half by the God Zeus. Each half is a twin flame who will forever search for its other half to complete them.

Twin flame relationships are intense soul connections. Your 'twin' is the person who can trigger you like no other. Often one person in the couple runs away from the relationship and the other pursues them – a stage known as the runner/chaser dynamic. Sound familiar?

Convinced that I had met the other half of my soul, I became obsessed with twin flame theory – reading books, watching YouTube videos and paying to consult self-proclaimed 'twin flame coaches'. There is a whole community of teachers online, dedicated to reuniting people with their supposed twins.

The dangerous thing about twin flame theory is that it normalises having a partner who runs from you or rejects you, making you feel that this is a natural stage of the 'twin flame journey' rather than identifying it as an unhealthy relationship. This keeps thousands of people (mainly women) existing in a state of perpetual hope that their twin will one day return to them.

During my time on the edges of the twin flame community, I saw many people who failed to move on from their twin years after the end of the relationship – even when their exes were married to other people or had started families. Twin flame coaches often encouraged them not to give up.

The more toxic behaviour I observed in my lover, the more convinced I became that he was my twin. I saw my own fears and insecurities mirrored in his, and any signs that he was pulling away from me were interpreted as him running from the intensity of our connection. I believed that if I healed myself, he would mirror that healing back to me and we would come into 'divine union'.

Whether this man was my twin flame or not, he was undoubtedly an amazing catalyst for my inner work. In retrospect, I believe that these twin flame relationships come into our lives to trigger our wounds and send us on a healing journey.

# ROCK BOTTOM

Meanwhile, my own life continued to spiral into chaos. My landlady told me she was evicting me from the house I'd rented with my ex-husband, plus I was being bullied at work and going through a stressful disciplinary procedure. My ex was angry to find out I was dating someone else and pledged to make my life hell, bombarding me with texts and emails about what a horrible person I was. My nervous system was in overdrive in constant fight or flight mode.

Despite this, I continued to act the role of saviour to my supposed twin, hoping he would recognise me for the wonderful, caring woman I was and reward me with the love that I so desperately craved. I was giving from an empty cup and things were reaching breaking point.

My coping strategies were alcohol and smoking – both things I'd seldom engaged in while married. Now I returned to the hedonistic lifestyle of my teens and early 20s. There was a sense of freedom as I would pour myself a vodka and Diet Coke and light up a cigarette in the evenings after the children had gone to bed. It felt like I was rebelling against my life as an unfulfilled wife and mother, returning to parts of myself I'd forgotten along the way.

I was getting in touch with the deep well of feelings that had been repressed for so long and were now being misguidedly projected onto my lover, who I believed was the cause of this emotional awakening. The feelings emerging were too much to bear and I was dulling them through pumping nicotine and alcohol into my body in an attempt to calm myself down. At that point in life, I had no other tools to cope. Escapism was the only route I knew.

Although the vodka sent me to sleep, I would wake in the middle of the night in panic attacks - gasping for breath with my heart pounding. I still remember how desperately lonely and hopeless I felt in those dark hours with the heavy responsibility of my two young daughters weighing upon me.

There was no obvious solution to any of my problems. I was completely saturated with a horrific and overwhelming fear. As far as I was concerned, I had messed up everything. I had failed at my marriage, life and career. I found myself at 35 renting a house I couldn't afford, a single mum, bullied by both my ex-husband and my boss, in a job I hated, exhausted and mentally unwell.

I must have brought this on myself, I reasoned, and I replayed my life critically trying to identify the moment I'd made the wrong turn that took me to this forlorn place. I'd obviously made a big mistake somewhere and I was full of self-hatred and regret.

One day, a friend who worked at the same newspaper as my lover called me out of the blue to say she had bad news. My heart sank as she told me that the man I believed was my twin flame was dating another woman in their office. Suddenly it made sense why he'd been acting so flaky. With shaking hands, I ended the call and texted him to say it was over between us.

Slumping back on the sofa, I felt as if I'd been punched in the gut. It hit me that I was totally alone. The terror I felt was hot, white and palpable. I couldn't go on as I was but had no idea how to turn things around.

In that despairing state, I began to silently plead for guidance. I'm not a religious person and had no idea who I was calling out for, but at that moment it felt like my last hope.

Suddenly, a memory arose from my jumbled brain. A few years previously, I'd attended a Buddhist meditation retreat with a friend. At the time, I'd considered it a weekend adventure, rather than something that could be part of my life. Now it randomly sprang to mind. Grabbing my laptop, I searched for the name of the retreat centre. Up popped a website offering several retreats from the Triratna Buddhist order. Instinctively, I knew it was exactly what I needed.

Scrolling through the site, I discovered the Taraloka centre for women on the border of Wales was holding a retreat soon. As synchronicity would have it, the children were due to go away on holiday with their dad the exact same week. All the pieces were coming magically together. With eyes still blurry from tears, I booked myself for seven days of meditation in the countryside. Whether it was my intuition, the Universe, or a higher power – it seemed my silent prayer had been answered.

## THE RELEASE

I rocked up at the Taraloka retreat centre in my colourful maxi dress, terrified about what lay ahead. As much as I needed to retreat from my life in London, the thought of a week meditating with strangers at an unfamiliar place filled me with trepidation. I'd been going out of my way to bury my pain and I knew that over the following days I would be forced to confront it.

Each day from 7am was spent in sessions of meditation, t'ai chi or talks about Buddhism. I learnt how to practise the body scan, mindfulness of breathing and Metta Bhavana (loving kindness) meditations. In between sessions I walked in the beautiful gardens or along the canal, relaxed in the living room or helped with cooking and cleaning tasks.

I journaled incessantly as emotion after emotion arose to be examined. My twin flame constantly inhabited my mind like a growing tumour and my body ached with the pain of missing him. Nobody ever tells you how much heartbreak physically hurts. I felt like a drug addict going through cold turkey withdrawal. One day I confided in one of the retreat's leaders that I wanted to let go of someone and asked for advice. Coincidentally (or not), the next day, she announced there would be a letting go ceremony during which we would burn something we wanted to release in an open fire.

In the retreat centre's art room that day I created a heart. The art room was full of paints, colours, cardboard and other materials to enable women to get in touch with their creative sides. I opted to make a collage. A copy of the very newspaper that my lover worked for happened to be in the room and I cut letters and words from it in the style of a poison pen letter to construct phrases that reminded me of him, things he had said to me and memories. As I cut and glued my makeshift heart like a four-year-old girl at nursery, I began to cry. That day I sobbed so much my body shook, and I could barely see what I was making. I was starting to let go of years of pent-up pain, disappointment and loss.

When evening fell, we gathered around the crackling campfire in the retreat centre's garden. There were around 20 women, each of whom was on their own personal journey of healing. Some were there because of relationship breakdowns, job losses or mental health issues, others were simply exhausted by life or searching for answers. Each held something in her hands that she wanted to let go of – mostly small pieces of paper with a few scrawled words.

I was the only one flamboyantly clutching an A4-sized pink painted heart embellished with newspaper cuttings. One by one we cast our offerings into the fire. Women were letting go of bad habits, talking unkindly to themselves, pushing themselves too hard, anger and sadness.

When it came to my turn, I stepped forward and announced I was letting go of the man who had broken my heart, before casting the beautiful piece of art that I'd wept over all day into the dancing flames. There was a round of applause and I received many pats on the back and hugs of support as everyone acknowledged my bravery. They had all been where I was. There is probably not a human on this Earth who won't experience heartbreak at some point and these women held the space for me as I let go of my pain.

We then chanted "Sabbe, sattā, sukhi, hontu" – a Pali chant that means 'May all beings be well'. Walking slowly around the grounds of the retreat centre in unison, we eventually came to encircle a statue of Tara, the female bodhisattva, which Taraloka is named after (Taraloka means Tara's realm). Legend has it that Tara was born from tears of compassion for all the suffering in the world. A deep feeling of peace came over me as I tuned into the energy of the women around me and all the others who had visited this retreat centre over the years – each of them with their own stories and pain. Held by their love, my heart began to heal. That was a magical evening.

## SOWING NEW SEEDS

The next day, the retreat leaders handed us each some ash from the remains of the fire and a few seed pods.

We were invited to plant seeds in the grounds to represent something new we wanted to grow in our lives. Immediately, I knew exactly where I wanted to plant mine. There was a secluded bench in the grounds where I often sat to journal. Its wooden surface bore a metal plate with the simple inscription 'Radiate Love'. I'd spent many hours over the last few days there, reading, writing and watching the white butterflies chasing each other.

Before planting my seeds, I wrote a heartfelt poem in my journal:

*'From these ashes I hope to grow something new,*

*I wish for love, I wish to accept myself,*

*I wish to dance and rejoice and feel*
*and trust again and not be scared,*

*So, I plant this seed pod to spread out into the world,*

*To heal my heart, to make something new,*
*to begin again, to feel hope.'*

A year later, I returned to the retreat centre to find that spot had become overgrown with wildflowers and wondered if some of them were from the seeds I planted that day. My life similarly started to bloom over that year, although there were still many more steps on my personal journey until I could really embody the vision in my poem.

At the time I wrote those words, they seemed so far away from my reality as to be a distant dream, but now I can honestly say they have become my reality. I have learnt to love and accept myself, and trust once more. Indeed, the dancing I longed for was to be a huge part of that journey, as you will find out later.

What I began to burn away in the fire that evening was not only that toxic twin flame love affair, but so many parts of who I thought I was and what my life would be. Over the coming years, I would be asked to let go of much more. In fact, I have let go of nearly everything of the person I once was.

Several years later, this letting go ritual is a regular part of the Awakening Women's Circles I co-run with a friend online. Each full moon we write out the things we want to let go of and burn them – just like I did that magical night at Taraloka.

# EMBODIMENT: BURN AWAY THE PAST

On the night of the full moon, safely light a small fire in a fireproof dish. Take a piece of paper and write down all the negative dating and relationship experiences from your past. Include any times you felt shame, judgement or rejection.

Close your eyes, visualise these situations and send love to them. Then cast the paper onto the fire and watch it burn away.

Repeat: "Under the light of the full moon, I release all that does not serve me."

If you're not able to safely light a fire, simply rip up the piece of paper and discard it.

Follow the ceremony by soaking in a salt bath using Epsom salts, sea salt, or Himalayan rock salt, imagining all the things you want to let go of being washed away. I personally like to change my sheets and get into a clean bed feeling purified of everything that has held me back.

This ceremony begins to clear the way to call new things into your life.

#Totallyloveable  @mindfuldivas

# LOVE JUNKIE

After returning home from retreat, I started to attend the London Buddhist Centre in Bethnal Green to take part in their weekly meditation classes.

One night, chatting with a woman I'd connected with, I told her about my failed marriage, followed by the heartbreak of my new relationship. Without missing a beat, she recommended I join a 12 Steps recovery programme for sex and love addiction.

I was horrified – wasn't sex addiction something that only celebrities like Russell Brand claimed to have? In my mind, it was associated with porn addicts, men who visited prostitutes, professional footballers and sex offenders. But the woman assured me that recovery groups were full of normal people who wanted to heal unhealthy relationship patterns. This was all very shocking to me, but as outlandish as it seemed, my intuition told me that I had been given an important message to take the next step on my path.

Anything that we consistently use to avoid, bury, or numb our pain is an addiction. Some people get their kicks from drugs, drink, compulsive shopping or overworking, I got mine from emotionally unavailable men. In that moment it hit me like a tonne of bricks – I was a love junkie. It was time to get clean.

When I got home, I searched online and found there were several 12 Steps groups that met in London. These meetings were like Alcoholics Anonymous, but rather than alcohol the substance of choice was love. Without a clue what I was letting myself in for, I decided to go along. Although meditation had helped me get more in touch with myself, I was still feeling hurt, angry and betrayed by men. I hoped the group could help me find some peace.

A code of confidentiality prevents me from saying too much about the group I joined, other than to say that if this calls to you, then please search online like I did for local organisations. What I can tell you is that it was the beginning of the deepest period of soul-searching of my life.

Firstly, I had to admit my life had become unmanageable because of my relationship addiction and trust that turning my life over to a higher power could restore me to sanity. This higher power could be God, the Universe, or anything else bigger than yourself.

The next step in the recovery programme was to make 'a searching and fearless moral inventory' of myself.

This involved writing a list of all my fears, resentments and times I'd caused harm to others. Believe me, this was a lengthy and painful process – one which I often wanted to avoid. But night after night I would sit and write these lists, remembering all the things that had hurt me throughout my life. These went right back from exchanges in the school playground to current things happening in my relationships and work. Nothing was spared from the lists, no matter how petty or irrelevant it seemed. If someone had so much as given me a backhanded compliment, let me down or offended me, I wrote it down.

Even worse was the list of times I'd hurt others – it was a sobering process to remember all the things I'd done, which at the time I had thought were justified. These included cheating on boyfriends, lying, talking behind people's backs, even incidents of name calling, violence and giving people the silent treatment. Each mean, thoughtless, unconscious act I had ever committed was brought back to life as I conjured up memories I'd deliberately pushed to the back of my mind in shame.

During this process, which took me a month, I completely stopped dating. I was so nervous that interacting with men would trigger my relationship addiction that I didn't even dare to go for a coffee with anyone male. Just like sobriety means not drinking for an alcoholic, for me it meant total abstinence from romantic temptation. Alcohol and cigarettes were also off the menu as I made the decision to stop dulling my pain with addictions and face up to the emotional baggage I'd been carrying for so many years.

If this exercise sound traumatic, it was! The most horrifying thing was that when the list of fears and resentments was finished, I had to read it to my 'sponsor', a seasoned member of the 12 Steps group who acted as my mentor.

It took me a gruelling eight hours sitting in a cafe to read out that list, as my sponsor listened to the seemingly endless litany of hurt, humiliation and shame. I'd like to say that after that I felt light and free, but I remember feeling exhausted and almost dirty. I hated admitting to all those dark parts of myself and now my sponsor knew everything bad about me.

As soon as I got home, I took a hot shower to wash away the experience, before collapsing into bed totally drained. It took a few days before the heaviness began to lift and I felt myself coming out on the other side. In some ways, I had energetically cleared this sludge from inside me and now I finally felt that I could move on from the shackles of the past.

# EMBODIMENT: FEAR INVENTORY

I don't expect you to undertake the intense process I went through to clear myself of the past, but there is an abridged version used in 12 Step programmes and other spiritual communities that may serve you just as well.

This fear inventory process can be used either as a daily practice or whenever you feel anxious about your love life (or anything else).

I recommend that you start with a list of all the fears you're carrying about your romantic life. Acknowledging these fears and bringing them into the light of day will stop them from festering inside you and blocking love from coming into your life.

**Step 1:** Choose who to address your inventory to. It could be your higher self, God, Goddess, the Universe, or whatever term resonates with you.

**Step 2:** Choose a resentment. This can be something about your love life which makes you feel sad, angry, anxious, or upset. For example, a situation with a lover or ex, or maybe a lack of dates or commitment. Whatever is relevant to your life right now.

**Step 3:** Write down all the fears behind this resentment. For example, if you're resentful about a man who didn't text you back or call you after a date, you might write: "I am resentful at my date because I have fear that I will never find the man of my dreams."

Then behind that fear there may even be a deeper fear such as: "I have fear that I am deeply unloveable".

That was a big one of mine. Dig deep and keep examining your fears.

**Step 4:** Once you've written out all your fears, you ask for these to be lifted by writing: "Dear [God/higher self/Universe/whoever you addressed the list to] I ask to be free of these fears and any others I cannot see, for the higher good of me and [insert the name of anyone else named in the inventory]."

**Step 5:** If you have a close friend or mentor who you can trust to be neutral then you could read this list out loud to them. This can also be done by leaving them a recorded voice message. They should not comment on what you share, only listen and thank you for your honesty.

**Step 6:** Rip up or burn the list of fears as a gesture to show you are willing to let go of them.

Here is an example:

Dear Universe,

I am resentful at the man I'm dating for not telling me that he loves me because:

I have fear that I will never find love.

I have fear that I will be alone forever.

I have fear of dying alone.

I have fear that no man will ever be good enough for me or be able to fulfil me.

I have fear that there is something fundamentally wrong with me.

I have fear that I need a man to make me happy.

I have fear that I can't be truly whole and fulfilled on my own.

I have fear that I will attend every wedding, birthday party and social occasion alone and be an object of pity.

I have fear that none of the other achievements I have made in my life count for anything unless I can get into a secure, stable partnership.

I have fear that I am pathetic and needy for wanting a relationship and love instead of being happy alone.

Dear Universe, I ask to be free of these fears and any others I cannot see for the higher good of me, my date and all others involved.

Love Tammy

As you can see, this exercise can go very deep and often reveals things that can feel shameful or embarrassing to admit – even to ourselves. This practice will be your constant and reliable companion along this journey of self-love, as it allows you to release and let go again and again.

#Totallyloveable @mindfuldivas

# LET GO OF DATING DISAPPOINTMENTS

When you're out there in the dating world it's easy to get discouraged. I know because I've been there! If you have a bad date, get ghosted or date someone who it doesn't work out with, please don't get disheartened. Return to the embodiment exercises in this chapter, identify the emotions and fears that come up for you and then let go. Everything that happens can reveal more about yourself and what you're looking for.

You have not failed. This is not a reflection on your worth, your lovability or your ability to call in the partnership you want. If you feel sad, angry or disappointed, that's OK. Society often encourages us to quickly move on with phrases such as 'he wasn't right for you' or 'you're better off without him', but these ignore the reality of our emotions and can make us feel ashamed of the depth of our feelings. Instead, treat yourself with a huge amount of compassion and hold space for whatever comes up for you without judgement.

## HEALING FROM NARCISSISTIC ABUSE

If, like myself and many of the women I work with, you identify as an empath, lightworker, or sensitive soul, you may have attracted a few narcissists in your time. These parasitic predators attach themselves to kind and forgiving people with weak boundaries. Before I give you any advice about dating, I feel it's my duty to warn you about these types, so that you can exercise due diligence and avoid trusting your precious heart with the wrong people.

It was reading the book *Psychopath Free* by Jackson MacKenzie that made me reflect on how toxic some of my past relationships had been. In my 20s I was engaged to a man who would fly into jealous rages and force to me to sleep on his bedroom floor as a punishment. Another long-term partner told me I was so repulsive that nobody other than him would ever want me. Looking back it's hard to believe my view of relationships was so skewed that I didn't instantly recognise that these behaviours were abusive.

By the term 'narcissist' I'm not referring to someone who is vain and self-centred (such as in the traditional story of Narcissus), but to someone with a narcissistic personality disorder. This is not about people who post too many selfies on Instagram. Narcissists have a grandiose sense of self-importance, little or no empathy, do not suffer remorse and have little regard for others' rights or emotions. They are often calculating but may hide this well and appear charming.

Obviously, it's unlikely that you will know if someone has a medical diagnosis of this type, and they probably won't have been diagnosed anyway. It is also not good to go around labelling anyone that treats you badly a narcissist – they may be good people who just have bad emotional or relationship skills. However, there are certainly warning signs to look out for.

# SIGNS OF NARCISSISTIC ABUSE:

- A partner who comes on very strongly initially, moves the relationship on quickly and seems to be the ideal partner you have always been looking for, before eventually becoming cold and withdrawn. This is called 'love bombing' and is how the narcissist initially hooks you in.

- Gaslighting – this is when someone tricks you into believing their version of reality against your own good judgement. They will even argue against things that you have seen with your own eyes/heard with your own ears, which makes you feel like you are going mad.

- Arguments that go on for hours without getting resolved. This is because the narcissist enjoys arguing and does not want to make up with you or find a compromise (even if they say they do).

- Gradually being cut off from friends and family. The narcissist will try to isolate you from your support network.

- Experiencing 'triangulation' when the narcissist uses a third party to make you feel jealous or insecure. For example, they may compliment other women, stay in contact with exes or flirt with others on social media. This can also take the form of them telling you that another person (such as their friend or mother) doesn't like you or is talking badly about you.

- You feel you must work hard for your partner's approval or validation or constantly justify yourself or your actions to them.

- You find yourself wishing your partner would go back to the kind, loving 'ideal partner' that they were in the beginning of your relationship.

- They can be very cruel to you and do not seem to care for your feelings, even though they may treat others kindly and appear a model citizen.

## IF YOU'RE IN LOVE WITH A NARCISSIST

The first thing you need to realise is that you can't change a narcissist and there is no known cure. It's important to cut this person out of your life and stop all contact. You need to come to terms with the fact that the 'perfect' partner you first met doesn't exist but was a false persona the narcissist adopted to attract you. It's like a mask they wear to disguise their true selves from the world. This may be hard to get your head around and you may find yourself longing for the person you initially thought they were. You may go through a grieving process as if that person has died.

The narcissistic relationship pattern is to idealise, devalue and then discard their partner. In other words, they initially build you up to be the most amazing person ever and put you on a pedestal. This is when you are new narcissistic supply, which feeds their ego and makes them look good to the world. They may also be using you to triangulate another partner or ex.

As time goes on, they will begin to lose interest in you as their new shiny object. Sometimes this happens because you do something to upset or offend them, which causes a blow to their ego, known as a narcissistic injury. It can be something as seemingly insignificant as disagreeing with them or praising someone else. This is when the devaluing begins and they start to find fault in everything you do, withdraw, or ignore you.

Often the victim of this behaviour will be confused and desperately trying to appease the narcissist to get back the relationship they used to have (which was actually fake). Eventually they will discard you by either ending the relationship, ghosting or making things so unpleasant that you are forced to leave.

Frequently, they will come back to you again after a few weeks or months when their egos need boosting, they're bored, they want to make a new partner jealous or need narcissistic supply. They will then tell you everything you want to hear to persuade you that the loving partner you originally fell for is finally back again. This process of returning is known as 'hoovering' because they attempt to suck you back in like a vacuum cleaner. Be aware that if you fall for this, they will eventually devalue and discard you again and this time the cycle will be shorter, and the discard will be more brutal. Partners stuck in this cycle can become entrenched in toxic and emotionally abusive on/off relationships for years.

Narcissists tend to identify your core wounds early in the relationship so that they can present themselves as the solution to all your problems. Later they will use these wounds to hurt you. For example, if you've been cheated on before, the narcissist will tell you that they abhor infidelity and would never be unfaithful to you. You will feel relieved and let your guard down, feeling that you have finally found someone you can trust. Later in the relationship, they will deliberately play on your fears by flirting with others or cheating on you. Their aim is to hit you where it hurts and cause the maximum damage so that you will be dependent on them.

I know this all sounds very disempowering and I don't like to present anybody as being a victim, which is why I am going to point out that you're not. If you're in a relationship with a narcissist, you must do the inner work and take responsibility for your part in the experience. For whatever reason, you looked for something outside of yourself which you thought the narcissist could give you. Maybe it was love, maybe it was approval, maybe it was status, or security or validation. That was how the narcissist lured you in.

It's time for you to identify how you can give that quality to yourself instead, then you will be able to free yourself from the clutches of the narcissist and make yourself immune to others. Once you realise that you don't really need the narcissist and they cannot and never could give you the thing you want, you'll be able to let go of your feelings for them.

Stop seeking their approval, stop arguing with them, stop trying to prove you are a good person or you're right. Just let go. Really and truly let go. Love yourself first instead. I know that sounds ridiculously simple and, if you're going through this situation right now, it will certainly not seem so easy. But I promise you that is the answer. How do I know? Because I have been there and done that.

When I was getting over my own toxic relationships, I took the Narcissistic Abuse Recovery Program (NARP) by Melanie Tonia Evans. She has also published a book which can go deeper into these issues.

## EMBODIMENT: WHAT NEEDS DOES THE NARCISSIST MEET?

Going to the narcissist to get your needs met is like going to a butcher to order a salad. It's simply not on the menu. However, at the start of your relationship, the narcissist doubtlessly made you feel that they could fulfil everything you ever wanted.

Now is the time to examine exactly what needs you thought they could meet. You will have to dig deep and be brutally honest for this process.

Write down your true feelings in your journal, in the knowledge that nobody else need ever read it. Some of your reasons may seem superficial or embarrassing, such as that you never thought a man so good looking would want to be with you, or you loved the fact he seemed affluent and took you out to impressive places that you'd never experienced before. Or maybe your reasons are more tender such as feeling that after so many men who only wanted sex, it was nice to finally meet someone who seemed interested in you as a person, or who said they wanted a family and kids like you do. The reasons will be your deepest and most secret desires.

**Part one:** Brainstorm everything that you felt you could get from this relationship.

Finish this sentence as many times as possible:

> I felt this relationship could give me ......
> because ......

For example:

> I felt this relationship could give me security because he is a successful businessman who seemed to be stable and want a family.

> I felt this relationship could give me passion and a good sex life because there seemed to be a spark between us.

> I felt this relationship could give me confidence in how I look because he was always giving me compliments.

> I felt this relationship could give me a sense of community and belonging because he seems to

be a popular person with lots of friends and I wanted to be a part of that.

Keep going until you've exhausted all the things you felt they could give you.

**Part two:** How can you meet your own needs?

Next, I want you to take each of those needs and write down at least one way you can give this need to yourself or get it met by other people or resources.

Finish this sentence as many times as you can:

I can give myself ...... [insert your need] by ......

For example:

I can give myself security by starting a savings account and putting away £100 of my earnings every month.

I can give myself passion and a good sex life by studying tantric self-pleasure practices.

I can give myself confidence in my looks by telling myself in the mirror each day how beautiful I look.

I can give myself a sense of community and belonging by signing up for a course I'm interested in where I can connect with like-minded people.

Obviously, this embodiment exercise won't immediately stop you longing for the narcissist, but in time, when you learn to meet your own needs, a partnership will become just one aspect of your life rather than a way of fulfilling it. This will make you less susceptible to becoming a target for narcissists in the future.

In a way, narcissists are an incredible gift in our life because they show us all the places we need to heal. As the Sufi poet Rumi said, the wound is the place where the light enters you.

#Totallyloveable  @mindfuldivas

## IDENTIFYING SAFE PEOPLE

Although in this book I encourage you to be vulnerable and open your heart, I recommend you use discernment in doing so. Your intuition can be a great guide in this. I know that many times I've ignored red flags in a partner because I didn't want to acknowledge them. Our inner voice is constantly giving us messages, so make sure to listen to these. As your self-worth rises, you'll be less likely to draw inappropriate people to you, as you'll be clearer about what you are looking for and quicker to notice and let go of anyone who doesn't meet your criteria.

Of course, not everyone who is not able to meet your needs is a narcissist – they simply may not be the right person for you at this time in your life.

Remember that safety is something you can create within yourself. When you truly love yourself, it doesn't matter so much how somebody else reacts to you because you're grounded in your own feelings of worthiness. This makes it possible to reveal your true self without fear and to know that the other person's reaction is their choice. When you can give yourself validation, it doesn't feel so important to gain it from others.

# CHAPTER TWO

# LOVE YOURSELF FIRST

"I wish I could show you,
When you are lonely or in darkness,
The Astonishing Light
Of your own Being!"
– Hafez

One of the clichés about being single I found the most annoying is that you need to love yourself first before someone else can love you. When I was single, that saying really got on my nerves for several reasons.

Firstly, I feared that maybe I couldn't love myself enough. Did that mean I was destined to be alone forever? This seemed desperately unfair – like a double punishment. As if not loving myself wasn't bad enough already!

Added to this was the frustration of seeing other people who didn't seem to love themselves but still had partners that loved them. How did they somehow manage to get around the rule? Yet another unfairness.

Also, I wondered what 'loving yourself' even meant and how I'd know when I achieved it? Some experts advocate self-care: bubble baths, buying yourself flowers and getting your nails done. Other people loudly proclaim that self-love is NOT about bubble baths and flowers – it's about tough inner work, facing your shadows, working with your demons and healing the past. Some say it's about repeating self-love affirmations in the mirror, while others say that affirmations will have no effect if deep down you don't really believe them. I felt confused by all of this.

I kind of loved myself, at least some days I thought I did. On other days I would spiral into self-hatred or shame and feel like I'd taken 10 steps backwards. Then I'd hate myself even more for ruining everything by not loving myself and therefore ruining the chance that anybody else could love me. I was stuck in a vicious circle of not loving myself for not loving myself and I didn't know how to get out of it.

It was my mindfulness practice that showed me the simple answer to this dilemma: self-compassion.

When I trained to be a mindfulness teacher, I started to learn about being kind to myself. It was something I'd heard about, maybe even something that I thought I already did. But now I started to discover what it meant on a much deeper level.

When I was on my introductory mindfulness teacher training retreat (which synchronistically was at the Taraloka retreat centre where my meditation journey had begun), I began to spiral down into a dark place. My mind was struggling to take on the self-concept of someone who could lead others as a teacher. I felt like I wasn't mindful, calm, serene or perfect enough. How could others possibly follow me when I didn't have everything in my own life together?

My sense of self was damaged and broken. I'd recently been made redundant from my job as a reporter. The severance pay had funded my mindfulness teacher training, but now I was worried about money, finding a new job and how I would support myself and my two children. I'd recently bought my first flat in

London through a shared ownership scheme (something which was a huge achievement for me as a single mum and first-time buyer), but I felt guilty that my daughters now had to share a bedroom and we no longer had a garden. My marriage had failed, my job had failed. Compared to many of my friends who had big houses, cars, high-flying jobs, and husbands, I felt like a loser.

During the training retreat we spent several days in silence, which meant that communication outside of the classroom was banned. This was intended to drop us deeper into our mindfulness practice and cut out any external distraction and chitter chatter.

On previous retreats, I'd enjoyed periods of silence and they'd helped me reach states of blissful peace. On my first retreat at Taraloka, I remember silently watching a bee flying from flower-to-flower contemplating how beautiful and complete nature was. All the pressures of my busy London life had dropped away and free from the pressure of socialising, I could have sat there for hours.

However, this retreat experience was to be very different. The silence only served to amplify the critical voices in my head. All I could think about was how inadequate I was for the role of mindfulness teacher, how I had failed at my life, and what a terrible mother I was.

Something more tender was also triggering me. I'd met a spiritual man on the retreat who was also training to be a mindfulness teacher. In my journal I reflected on what a wonderful, kind, caring man he was – unlike the self-centred, sex-obsessed guys I usually met through online dating. It seemed there was a connection between us and I sensed that he felt the same way.

One night on a mindful poetry evening we curled up besides each other on the sofa chatting about life. I was feeling happy and warm, basking in the light of his attention when he casually dropped his girlfriend into the conversation. Not only that - they lived together and were trying for a baby. The revelations kept coming like mini bombs exploding. Although I tried to act unbothered, I felt a red flush of humiliation spread up my neck and cheeks. Embarrassed that he might see my reaction I turned away from him to talk to someone else, pushing him away as I had so many other men who had hurt me in the past.

This may seem like an insignificant incident, but for me it was further confirmation of how totally unloveable I was. Secretly I had hoped to meet a conscious partner on the retreat and when I met this handsome kind-hearted stranger, I thought my fantasy was coming true. Instead, I now felt rejected and ashamed. I angrily berated myself for thinking a man like that would want someone like me. Are you getting a sense of how unkind to myself I was back then? As far I was concerned the Universe most definitely didn't have my back (sorry Gabrielle Bernstein!).

On the teacher training course we'd been learning how to lean into painful sensations, and I knew that mindfulness meant paying close attention to your emotions. Attempting to be a model student, I desperately tried to stay with my feelings of shame, hurt and failure.

As silence echoed around the retreat centre, I found myself facing a dark night of the soul, with nobody to confide in or console me. In retrospect, after having trained in trauma-sensitive mindfulness, I can see that buried trauma was surfacing from the difficulties I'd been through – the divorce, failed relationships, moving house, redundancy and family problems.

I'd experienced some of the most stressful experiences a human can have over the last few years, so it wasn't surprising that now I stopped to pay attention to myself I was flooded with painful emotions. My thoughts were so unrelentingly dark and my body aching with such agony that it crossed my mind that I couldn't go on. I was meant to be stepping into this exciting new role as a mindfulness teacher but all I wanted to do was die. My wounds, insecurities and fears were coming to the surface to be healed, and it felt unbearable.

One icy afternoon at my lowest ebb, I sat shivering on the same 'Radiate Love' bench where I'd planted the seeds a few years back, but now I was doing anything but radiating love. Instead, I was writing in my journal about my emotional pain. This bench was usually my happy place, but today I was overcome with depression.

A figure approached me – it was a woman who was doing the advanced teacher training course in another part of the retreat centre. I won't go into her personal circumstances as that's not my story to tell, but she'd been through many hardships of her own before discovering mindfulness. Now she was full of light and acted as an inspiration for others. Despite the silence we were bound to, she came to speak to me. To my surprise, she asked if she could give me a hug and told me I was beautiful inside and out and she loved being around me.

I was taken aback by this unexpected display of kindness. Little did she know how well-timed her words were and how much I needed that hug. It was as if she was an angel sent to save me in that dark moment and I remain eternally grateful for the impact her actions had on me that day. It turned out the Universe did have my back after all.

A popular definition of mindfulness from the well-known teacher Jon Kabat-Zinn is: "the awareness that arises from paying attention, on purpose, in the present moment and non-judgmentally".

In paying close attention to my feelings, I'd forgotten the non-judgemental part. I was judging myself for everything I perceived I'd ever done wrong in my life and all the many ways I felt I'd messed up. But this kind act from a near stranger reminded me of the essential element I'd been neglecting in my mindfulness practice: compassion.

# EMBODIMENT: MIRROR WORK

It's so common to speak to ourselves in a way we would never dare to speak to anyone else. Are you ever flooded with negative thoughts, feelings and beliefs about yourself or your ability to find love? Maybe you're haunted by the failures of past relationships, regrets and things you felt you did wrong. If you are, I know exactly what you are going through, and I want to promise you that this can change.

Decide to be your own best friend – look in the mirror and say exactly the opposite to whatever those negative thoughts in your mind are telling you. If your mind is telling you you're too old or too unattractive to find love, then look yourself in the eyes and tell yourself the opposite.

If your mind is telling you that you're unloveable, a loser and nobody will ever want you, then tell your reflection that you're loving and loveable, beautiful, deeply attractive and anyone would be lucky to be with you – just like you would talk to a friend who needed reassurance.

This may feel strange or awkward at first but do it anyway. It's important that you learn to love yourself ferociously and putting yourself down cannot be tolerated under any circumstances. If you continue with this practice, talking to yourself lovingly will soon become second nature.

I say something loving to myself pretty much every time I see my reflection these days. Usually something playful with a wink. When you start to give yourself love, your energy will vibrate at that level and others will see you through the eyes of love too – including your ideal partner.

#TotallyLoveable    @mindfuldivas

## KNOW THYSELF

Part of the journey of attracting a loving partner is deeply knowing yourself. By this, I'm not talking about any of the external factors such as your job, appearance, past relationships or financial situation. I mean really getting to know your inner self, so that your soulmate can recognise you.

What we experience internally is often reflected externally in our lives. Before I got into a happy relationship, I spent a lot of time reconnecting with myself and the things that inspired me.

Connecting with yourself is like turning on a brilliant light that allows you to be seen, effortlessly putting your life on track to be in the right place at the right time. This is a magical process that leads you to the experiences most needed for your self-growth. It was this process that led me to an amazing synchronicity.

One stage of the Metta Bhavna meditation involves directing loving kindness towards someone neutral. This person can be a casual acquaintance – maybe a shopkeeper or someone who works in your office whom you seldom talk to, someone you have no real relationship with or strong feelings about either way.

When I learnt this meditation on retreat at Taraloka, I looked around the room and randomly picked a woman with purple hair, who I hadn't interacted with much. That week she became my designated neutral person and each day in the meditation I focused my loving kindness on her, repeating the phrases: 'May you be well, may you be happy, may you be free from suffering, may you be loved.'

Little did I know that several months later this loving kindness would come right back at me.

For many years I've had a rule that if I'm told about something three times, I act on it. Hearing something that intrigues me once is interesting, twice is a message, but the third time I take as a very clear sign. This method has led me to many interesting places and situations.

In the months following my first retreat, I'd adjusted to my new lifestyle of regular meditation and began spending time with new circles of people who were spiritual and conscious. A couple of times I heard mentions of 5Rhythms – an ecstatic dance practice devised by Gabrielle Roth in which you move through five types of music known as a wave. Each stage of the music represents a different state of consciousness: flowing, staccato, chaos, lyrical and stillness.

I'd always loved dancing, but since my partying days were largely over, I didn't get much chance anymore. What sounded amazing about this practice was that it was not only a dance, but a way to express and process emotions.

Although 5Rhythms seemed like something I could enjoy, it was also out of my comfort zone. The thought of turning up to a room of strangers to dance my heart out filled me with a sense of self-conscious dread.

One night I went out for dinner for a friend's birthday. This was unusual as I still wasn't drinking alcohol and hadn't been socialising much to avoid temptation. But the occasion was a close friend's 30th, so I wasn't going to miss the celebration.

We met in an Indian restaurant, and I got chatting to the woman sitting next to me. She began telling me about how she practised... you guessed it, 5Rhythms! It was a complete chance meeting as our mutual friend wasn't particularly spiritual or into that kind of thing. But, of course, I don't believe in coincidences – this was happening for a reason. It was the third time I'd heard the message and now I knew that inhibitions or no inhibitions I had to act.

After I expressed my interest in 5Rhythms, the woman invited me along to a dance happening the following weekend. I jumped at the chance, and a few days later, we danced the evening away together at a one-off event in London.

I loved the night and, eager for more, I decided to go along to a weekly class in the East End of London, run by a well-respected 5Rhythms teacher. When I turned up on a Sunday night to a church hall in Bethnal Green, I was momentarily stunned. The teacher was none other than the purple-haired 'neutral person' I'd sent my love to on retreat! Yet another huge synchronicity signalling I was on the right path.

Over the next year that 5Rhythms class became my saviour as I attended each week and eventually became part of the crew, assisting the teacher by taking money at the door, setting up the room and cleaning up afterwards.

I danced so many emotions on that church hall floor– pounding out my anger, fear, pain, hope and love – often reaching ecstatic states of bliss. Through dancing, I expressed the things that couldn't be said in words. The music became my medicine.

The purple-haired teacher held space at the class with sensitivity and grace and the music was always perfect to let go of whatever emotion I needed to release. Sometimes during the dance, I would feel such immense gratitude for being there in that space that I would silently thank the teacher for being born. I was so in awe of her that we barely spoke a word to each other, but she remains one of my most significant mentors.

Remembering this story, I'm still blown away by the synchronicities that led me to that healing journey, but even more so the way the love I put out into the world through meditation returned and blessed my life in such an unexpected way.

# EMBODIMENT: DANCE
# YOUR EMOTIONS

You may want to check if there are any 5Rhythms or other ecstatic dance classes in your area or that you can attend online. If there are, I highly recommend them for releasing trapped emotions, discovering yourself and self-expression. But even if there isn't a class, you could try this simple practice at home.

Identify how you're feeling today. Put your hand on your heart and feel into your body for any emotions. Once you've got in touch with your mood, choose a piece of music that embodies that. I've created playlists on Spotify for different moods so I can always find the perfect music to dance to.

Put on the music and dance like nobody is watching (hopefully they aren't). As you dance, stay in tune with your breath. If feelings arise, let them come – cry, laugh, howl, roar. Let everything release.

#TotallyLoveable    @mindfuldivas

# LOVE IN LOCKDOWN

The coronavirus lockdown of 2020 may have been a nightmare in many ways, but it was a perfect time for developing self-love. As we weren't even allowed out of the house, dating became impossible and single people were forced into involuntary solitude and celibacy. Strangely, this felt like a relief, and I surrendered completely to the situation. It was like the pressure of dating had been lifted. Instead of feeling my usual loneliness, I felt a sense of solidarity knowing that so many others were also alone. With no other option, I put all my effort into caring for myself.

During lockdown, my 5Rhythms classes went online, and I started to take part regularly to relieve the tension and anxiety of the pandemic. Surprisingly, the practice was still very powerful at home without the physical presence of the group.

Usually in a class we'd be instructed to take a partner at certain points, but obviously that wasn't an option for anyone living alone. Yet one evening while dancing, I caught my own reflection in the window and began to dance with myself. Instead of looking at myself with critical eyes to assess my outfit or figure, I took delight in myself as a partner. I noticed how fun and playful I was to dance with. Making different shapes with my body I delighted in the way they were reflected straight back to me. I smiled at myself and enjoyed the sight of the face smiling back at me from the reflection. Maybe it was the extreme isolation of lockdown, but it was the first time that I truly recognised myself as a friend.

When it comes to loving yourself, it can seem like an impossible mission – something that requires an arduous journey of work, healing, and effort. But sometimes it really is as simple as enjoying your own face smiling back from the mirror.

When you think of someone in your life you care for and enjoy spending time with, you don't have to make a huge effort to feel a sense of happiness. Nor do you need that person to be perfect. Just being with a friend or loved-one, chatting, watching a movie, or eating some food can feel deeply nourishing. I challenge you to start seeing yourself as a friend and bring that same sense of gentle, warm, effortless love and kindness to yourself.

This sparked an idea about having a love affair with myself. In *The Artist's Way*, Julia Cameron's classic book about creativity, she recommends a practice of taking yourself on an artist's date each week. This is anything you want to do just for the pleasure of it. The rule is that you go alone and don't let anyone else hijack your date with yourself. It's part of a process of learning to trust yourself, know yourself and love yourself more.

## EMBODIMENT: TAKE
## YOURSELF ON A DATE

What would you most like to do? Don't wait for someone else to do it with – put it in your diary and commit to doing it today. The only rule is that you must do this activity alone.

If you need some inspiration, here are some of the artist's dates I've been on:

- A walk in a beautiful park or garden
- Reading a book, journaling, or people watching in a favourite cafe
- Going to see a play
- Watching a movie matinee in the afternoon and eating chocolate popcorn (the popcorn was to make it seem extra indulgent)
- Exploring a new area
- Eating dinner in a favourite restaurant
- A spa day
- Lying in a local park sunbathing and reading

I learnt an interesting fact about artist's dates. I took part in a webinar with Cameron and one of my favourite authors, Elizabeth Gilbert. I discovered that Gilbert's best-selling memoir *Eat, Pray, Love* was inspired by *The Artist's Way*.

Gilbert said that when she looked back at her morning pages (a practice Cameron advocates of freestyle writing every morning) she realised that she'd repeatedly written about wanting to learn Italian. Her trip to Rome documented in the book was an artist's date that led her to inspiring millions of women.

#TotallyLoveable    @mindfuldivas

## ON BEING CHOSEN

As a child, there was a tortuous weekly ritual that I hated. Shivering with humiliation in my uniform PE knickers on the school field, we would line up to be picked for sports teams.

In winter it was for hockey or netball, in summer for rounders. But the one thing all these sports had in common was that I was terrible at them. I somehow lacked any hand-eye coordination or running ability.

Consequently, I was always picked last. Every single time.

Each moment waiting for my name to be called was another humiliation. I silently willed the ground to open up and swallow me, rather than stand there exposed and unchosen.

I wonder if PE teachers knew how damaging this is to children's self-esteem they would stop this cruel procedure? Many nights' sleep was lost worrying about school the next day, trying to devise a way to get out of PE class.

If only I could be thinner, faster, sportier, more coordinated, more popular, I thought. Then they would like me, then they would choose me. My innocent childhood mind reasoned there must be something terribly wrong with me to be picked last every time. That feeling of not being chosen stayed with me throughout adult life. I feared I would not be chosen by friends, by employers and by men. And, of course, that's what manifested.

Do you relate? Maybe you were good at sports, but there was another area you didn't feel chosen in. Maybe you weren't 'the clever one', 'the pretty one' or in some other way you felt like an outsider.

As an adult, you get to stop waiting to be chosen and choose yourself. Decide that you are the one who gets to have an amazing life and love. Stop waiting for something outside yourself to validate you. Decide right now that you are more than worthy of everything you desire. Don't wait for anyone else. You are the one you've been waiting for.

## EMBODIMENT: CHOOSE YOURSELF

Journal about your current romantic situation and go deep. If you feel unloved, examine where else you've felt like this in your life. When were you not picked? Where are you not choosing yourself?

Use art to express your feelings – if you're a writer then write your emotions into a poem or story, if you're an artist then paint or draw them, if you're a singer then sing them, if you're a dancer then dance them out. Let these feelings be transmuted into something beautiful.

Don't focus on the story of being not chosen, simply focus on the feelings this brings up for you. Speak to yourself soothingly like you would a child who was hurting. Make loving yourself and being with yourself

compassionately your number one priority. Decide
that from now on you get to choose yourself.

#TotallyLoveable    @mindfuldivas

# CHAPTER THREE

## MINDFULLY MANIFEST LOVE

"Stop trying to change the world since it is only the mirror.
Man's attempt to change the world by force is as fruitless
as breaking a mirror in the hope of changing his face.
Leave the mirror and change your face."
– Neville Goddard, Your Faith is Your Fortune

The Law of Attraction, made mainstream in 2006 by Rhonda Byrne's book *The Secret*, is the theory that we attract people, situations and things to us by our thoughts. In short, it's the idea that thoughts become things. This process of deliberately creating our lives is also known as manifestation.

However, this theory also throws up some problems. It can make people feel that they should be positive all the time to manifest what they want or even feel scared they'll mess up their manifestations if they experience negative thoughts or feelings.

For many years I tried Law of Attraction techniques to no avail. Even though I followed the techniques in *The Secret* and other books, I couldn't seem to manifest what I wanted. This was especially true when it came to love.

No matter how much I visualised my perfect partner, said positive affirmations or wrote lists describing the attributes of my dream man, it didn't seem to happen. After my divorce, I met so many men who weren't right for me that I began to wonder if manifestation was even possible or if it was a ploy invented to sell books. As you can tell, my mind wasn't in a very positive place for calling in love!

It was only after training in mindfulness that I began to see results and realised the incredible link between mindfulness and manifesting.

## WHAT'S MINDFULNESS ANYWAY?

In my work teaching mindfulness, I hear a lot of uncertainty about what mindfulness is. It's frequently confused with 'mindset', which is the way you think about and see things. Also, people some-times have misconceptions that mindfulness is about keeping your mind empty of thoughts, or that it's a technique that you 'do'.

It's not surprising there's some confusion, because mindfulness is simultaneously both a simple and a profound concept.

At its heart, mindfulness is simply just being. Prac-tices such as meditation, focusing on an activity or being aware of the breath can allow us to experience this state, but those practices themselves are not mindfulness. Mindfulness is, in my opinion, the true beauty of who you are with nothing added or taken away. It's your pure essence without beliefs, stories, obsessions or a constantly chattering mind. It's the state of feeling fully alive, present, awake, and aware.

We are all born naturally mindful. Babies live in the moment – they cry when they're hungry, sleep when they're tired and laugh when they're happy. They look into people's eyes deeply with curiosity and without self-consciousness.

If you go for a walk with a toddler, you'll see how aware of their surroundings they are. They express wonder and fascination at everything they see, whether it's a flower, a bee, or a puddle. I remember feeling frustrated at the slow pace of trying to get my daughter to nursery as she would constantly stop to examine things. A toddler's pace doesn't take into consideration the hectic demands of adult life in modern-day society. What would it be like to experience the world like a toddler again? To feel wonder at the sky, the sounds of nature, the thunder and rain? That is mindfulness.

## THE MISSING LINK
## TO MANIFESTING LOVE

At first glance, mindfulness and manifestation may seem to be opposite concepts. Mindfulness is about living in the present moment and accepting all your experience without judgement, whereas manifesting is about getting what you want in the future.

So how can being present in the moment help you to manifest what you want? In my mindfulness training courses I teach about a concept called the 'paradox of mindfulness'. This is the idea that to get to somewhere you want to go you must first fully accept where you are. This is a radical proposition in a world in which we're taught to push our way ahead using pure discipline and willpower.

I grew up in the 1980s, when aerobics was becoming popular, along with slogans such as 'feel the burn' and images of Jane Fonda in a leotard and neon leg warmers. It was seen as necessary to push yourself as hard as possible to get results. This tends to be a common mentality when trying to achieve something, whether it be a fitness goal, a new job or finding a relationship.

Yet anyone who has spent a lifetime yoyo dieting can tell you that willpower alone doesn't get you to your goals, because eventually it subsides, and you end up giving in to those chocolate cravings and falling back to square one, feeling like a failure. This is the 'boom/bust cycle' – an endless merry-go-round of pushing hard to achieve goals, followed by exhaustion and relapse. Then there are feelings of guilt and the determination to do better next time.

This cycle can repeat itself infinitely and each time there are stronger feelings of failure. Eventually you may burn out, come to believe that you simply lack enough willpower to achieve your goals and become resigned to never obtaining the things you desire.

Mindfulness is a completely different approach. Instead of exerting effort to get to an imaginary future in which you have your dream life, you practise accepting and appreciating where you are right now – including both the unpleasant and pleasurable aspects of your experience. Like many things in mindfulness (and in life), there is an inherent contradiction involved.

When you put your attention on 'getting' something you want, it only emphasises that you don't have that thing and puts you into a state of lack. This creates resistance to what you want.

In contrast, when you're mindful, you become aware that many aspects of what you want are already present in your experience and you start tending to those, like watering newly growing shoots. Eventually, those fresh young shoots can bloom into fully-fledged flowers and your current reality will be transformed in beautiful ways.

So, how does this concept relate to love and relationships? When it comes to love, if we try too hard to meet our goals, it can work against us. Love is not and should never be hard work. If you put in a large amount of effort, you're effectively transmitting the message to the Universe that this part of your life is difficult and the results you get back will reflect this.

Many things happen easily every day without having to worry about them – the sun comes up, the world turns, and your breath continuously flows. To effortlessly manifest love, you need to trust, let go and feel confident enough to stop pushing so hard. If you were truly content with where you are, then you wouldn't need to put in a huge effort.

This concept is hard to get your head around, I know – that's why it's called a paradox! But haven't you heard people say things like: 'when you stop looking for love is when you'll find it'?

This is exactly why. When we are viewing something as a problem to be overcome, we attract more problems to us. What we resist persists and if we focus on the lack of love, we will experience even more lack.

So, what's the alternative? With mindful manifestation, we set our intention and then simply know that it is done. Then we relax and practise being present in the moment – accepting and appreciating our life exactly as it is. You'll find that resistance comes up and that's a good thing, because it shows you any blocks and limiting beliefs you have so that you can clear them.

During this process, you don't have to feel positive or act in any particular way. It's vitally important that you fully experience all of your feelings and don't try to ignore any sadness, anger or doubt that arises. This process is about being real, true to yourself and authentically you. It doesn't involve pushing past pain barriers, forcing yourself to be smiley and upbeat 24 hours a day or feeling guilty if you are not constantly full of the joys of spring. There is no strategy. This is about being real.

It may be hard to believe you can get what you want without trying hard because it goes against the social conditioning you've most likely received throughout your life. Just think about how many messages you've received since childhood that you must work hard to get what you want. How would it feel to let go of all that pressure?

## THE LAW OF ASSUMPTION

There are a lot of confusingly different teachings about what you need to do to manifest what you want through the Law of Attraction. Some teachers say that you must feel the feeling of having what you want, some say you can never utter any negative words, some that you need to act as if you already have what you want.

I once followed the advice of a book which said that to manifest my dream partner, I should set up my home as if I was already living with him. Maybe you've also read advice to set two places at the table at mealtimes and pretend your soulmate is there eating with you? Well, this book recommended keeping one drawer empty for your future husband and emptying half your wardrobe to give him enough space. It even suggested leaving different coloured coat hangers out for your imaginary partner.

Diligently, I went out and bought pink coat hangers for me and grey for him. I cleared out half of my wardrobe (having to double hang many of my clothes) and displayed my future love's grey coat hangers on the other side of the wardrobe. I also cleared out the top drawer on one side of the bed, considerately leaving it clear for my soulmate to store his stuff. Now I had built our perfect love nest, surely he would come?

Well, no, it didn't work out that way and, after a few weeks, I got sick of having all my clothes squashed on one side of the wardrobe and not having enough storage space. I stole my imaginary lover's grey coat hangers for myself and reclaimed my bedside drawer. I may not have met my husband, but at least I had enough room for my clothes.

As far as I'm concerned, setting up your house as if your future partner lives there is missing the point. There are many other similar recommendations from manifestation teachers, such as the 369 method, the 5x55 method, or the two-cup method. You can look up all these online if you're curious, but I'm not going to teach any of them in this book. In my opinion, the secret to manifestation is very simple – it's a matter of believing that you can have what you want and that it's already done.

As well as the Law of Attraction, I'm a believer in the Law of Assumption, which was taught by the early 20th century spiritual leader Neville Goddard. This is the belief that our reality is created by our own consciousness. So, rather than attracting things to us, we're creating our lives and everything in them through our perception. This means that anything we manifest doesn't interfere with others' free will because they only exist within our perceived reality anyway.

By assuming that what you want is already true, it will harden into reality. Manifestation is the after-effect of materialisation in consciousness. In other words, you have to believe it before you see it. It doesn't matter how you feel or what the external circumstances are – even if you've spent another night alone in front of the TV, had a bad date or been dumped. You keep assuming everything is working out for you to get what you want, regardless of external evidence.

It's important to imagine what the result of your manifestation will feel like. Goddard calls this 'living in the end'. For example, if you want to be married, imagine how it would feel to be married – even for a few seconds. See a scenario in your mind's eye that represents how you want your marriage to be and allow yourself to enjoy the pleasurable sensations in your body. Smile and know it is done.

If it helps, you can script (write down) exactly what you want to happen. When you find yourself feeling upset or doubting because you haven't seen physical evidence of what you're manifesting yet, think or say out loud: "Even when I feel sad or doubt my manifestation, I still know that it's true. My feelings don't affect my manifestation."

And because you are the creator of your own reality, this will be true. To learn more about the Law of

Assumption, I suggest researching the work of Neville Goddard, but if you only do the basic steps I've outlined, you'll see things start to happen.

I put this into effect in my own life to attract back a partner after we broke up. I imagined us together and assumed he wanted to be with me. Any time I felt doubt I would say to myself that he missed me and was thinking of me. One of my main assumptions was that every time I thought about him, he was thinking about me too. Within six months, we were back together, and he told me he'd been thinking about me all the time. This stuff works!

## EMBODIMENT: KNOW YOUR OWN POWER

To manifest love, it's important to be clear about what you want. Script a 'love list' in the present tense of things you desire. As you write, let the desires channel through you and feel the relief of expressing what you want. Don't hold anything back.

Read through your list frequently (at least twice a day plus any time you feel low or need a boost).

Personally, I keep my lists on locked notes on my iPhone so that they're always available to me. I also jot down affirmations in any spare moments I get. If negative beliefs and feelings emerge, I write the opposite of them. Believe that everything you've written is true.

Here is an example list:

> I am loved.
> I am desired.
> I'm the love of my man's life.
> He wants to be with me night and day.
> My man is so considerate and kind.
> My man is so loving and caring.
> I feel so blessed to have my beautiful man.
> My man feels so blessed to have me.
> We're so happy to have our loving, caring relationship.

Get the picture? Just carry on like this using the words and phrases that resonate most with what you want. Don't make this something that feels like boring or like a chore. This is a fantasising exercise and should feel fun, light and enjoyable. These lists are powerful and if you trust in the process, you'll soon find that everything you've written has become your reality.

#TotallyLoveable    @mindfuldivas

# CHANGE YOUR SELF-CONCEPT

An important element often omitted about manifestation is that you must believe you're the person who can have the things you want. In other words, you need to change your self-concept.

If you want more money, you can't hold the belief that you're poor, or if you want to win the lottery, you can't believe you're unlucky. Likewise, if you're manifesting a new relationship, you must believe you're the person who can have the love you desire in your life. You need to know that you are loveable, valuable and worthy.

Where people often go wrong is coming up with justifications for this – for example, writing a list of reasons you're a good catch. There's nothing wrong with this in theory if it bolsters your self-esteem, but the truth is that you're still looking for external factors for validation. Think about it; if you truly felt loveable, you wouldn't need to write a list like that in the first place!

You need to know beyond doubt that you're worthy of love regardless of your looks, qualifications, body type, bank balance, job status or relationship history. You're worthy just because you exist. You don't have to be perfect to be loved. Let me repeat that because it's maybe the most important sentence you'll read in this book: *You don't have to be perfect to be loved.* This concept was a revelation for me, and it may be for you too.

If you've been reading every self-help book about relationships, trying to get the perfect body, constructing the most enticingly seductive texts, planning dazzling outfits and practising your witty banter, let me tell you now, it's all unnecessary.

Of course, better yourself in life for yourself because you love learning, taking care of your body, looking your best, or whatever it may be. But don't do it because you think it will help you attract love. All you need to do to attract your ideal partner is to believe that you're already enough because you are. As soon as you realise this, the evidence will manifest in the external world.

I hold the belief that my partner is attracted to me however I look and that he loves all the things I find unattractive about myself. This manifests for me daily. He likes my curves, my wrinkles, my cellulite, my scars, my messy hair in the morning, the weird face I pull while I'm sipping my tea. He loves everything about me because I created my relationship to be that way. How do you achieve this? Simply by believing it. When you say or script affirmations for what you want to manifest, make sure to include some that relate to your self-concept.

## EMBODIMENT: AFFIRMATIONS FOR AMAZING SELF-CONCEPT

Write a list of statements in the present tense as if you're the person who has what you desire. You already are this person, but maybe you don't believe it yet.

As you write the words, know they are true. You bring what you want into being simply by knowing it to be true regardless of any outside proof. It really is that easy.

For example:

> I am the woman who has the life and
> relationship of her dreams.
> All my relationships are healthy and happy.
> My partner loves and adores my body.
> My partner thinks I'm the most beautiful woman
> in the world.

I am loved.
I am loveable.
I am wanted.
I am desirable.
I have the life of my dreams.
Everything is always working out for me.
Everything in life goes in my favour.
I'm a lucky person.
My life is abundant.

Get it? Now you have a list of affirmations for what you want and a separate list for who you are. Read both these lists regularly and add to them every day or whenever the whim takes you.

I recommend repeating them as you look in the mirror. Most of all, believe in what you have scripted. If you hear the voice of doubt arising, tell it to pipe down. You've got this!

If the affirmations really don't feel true to you try starting each one with "I intend that...'.

In the following chapters, I'll provide you with more techniques for dealing with the negative voices that can arise when we try to call in our desires.

#TotallyLoveable     @mindfuldivas

## STAY IN THE VIBRATION OF LOVE

Once you've set your clear vision for what you want and believe you are the person who can have it, you can sit back and relax, knowing that your manifestation is done. Remember you never have to do anything or work hard to deserve love. Love is your birthright.

Keep holding the vision of what you want. Know with all your heart that it exists, and it is already yours. Make the picture of what you desire as big, beautiful and vibrant as possible in your mind. When Neville Goddard talks about living in the end, it means really believing that your wish has come true.

It's possible to have what you want – all of it. If you believe you're creating your reality, then you can create the relationship and love of your dreams. When something in your dating life appears to go wrong, identify any negative beliefs that came up, make adjustments and return to your vision. You are fine-tuning your dream so that when it manifests into reality, it will be more amazing than you could ever have imagined.

During this time, it helps to stay in the vibration of love as much as possible. This means choosing love over fear whenever doubts arise. By staying in a loving place, you're aligned with manifesting the love you desire, and this helps it come to you in the easiest and most effortless way.

## EMBODIMENT: BE THE LOVE
## YOU WANT TO SEE IN THE WORLD

Focus on anything which helps you feel loving. This can include doing random acts of kindness for others such as letting someone go ahead of you in a queue or phoning an elderly relative you haven't spoken to in a long time. Watch uplifting movies, read love stories and listen to upbeat songs.

Another way to stay in the vibration of love is to repeat the Ho'oponopono prayer. This is a Hawaiian prayer, which was made famous by Dr Hew Lenby and Joe Vitale. The words are simple:

*I love you*
*Please forgive me*
*Thank you*
*I love you*

Repeating this again and again is very soothing. I've also found recordings of this on YouTube and when I need to get into the vibration of love, I listen to them on repeat as I go about my day.

#TotallyLoveable    @mindfuldivas

# CHAPTER FOUR

# DITCH THE OLD STORY

"I am not what happened to me,
I am what I choose to become."
– Carl Jung

Neville Goddard has a wonderful expression that I live by: "Let the old man die." It may sound a bit cruel, but don't worry, it's not talking about somebody's grandad. The old man is a metaphor for all the thoughts and beliefs that no longer serve you.

Many of us walk around carrying negative stories about ourselves. You may believe that you always date losers, end up in the friend zone or that you're too old to find love. But to manifest an amazing love story, you must be willing to say goodbye to these outdated concepts of yourself. This can be easier said than done – the stories we tell can often seem so real that we believe them to be true. If we're not aware of these beliefs, they tend to run the show.

As the legendary psychoanalyst Carl Jung said: "That which we do not bring to consciousness appears in our life as fate."

Even if we're aware of our old stories, there may be a secret payoff we get for sticking to them. This payoff could be sympathy from friends, playing the victim or not having to go through the discomfort of putting ourselves out there on the dating scene again. But, if we are to free ourselves from the shackles of limitations, we need to reject any negative story we tell about ourselves.

## MOULDY CAKE

Trying to manifest love (or anything else) when we're holding onto old stories, negative beliefs and pain is a bit like putting a big dollop of icing sugar on a mouldy cupcake. It may look good but when you take a bite there'll be no hiding that it's rancid.

Likewise, we may try to 'think positive' and focus on what we want, but if underneath the positivity there are a lot of festering beliefs, you won't be able to manifest what you want. That's why it's so important to let the old stories go.

Many manifestation teachers speak about staying in the right vibration and not acknowledging any opposition. This led to me desperately trying to smile all the time, pushing any negative thoughts out of my mind, constantly repeating affirmations and doing anything I could to stay high vibe.

The problem is that humans are not one-dimensional beings who are constantly upbeat. We are multi-faceted beings with a myriad of emotions, and this is something beautiful to be embraced. Women are cyclical beings, our bodies and moods changing with the moon and tides of the sea each month.

By repressing my sad, angry, confused and scared feelings, I simply pushed them down deep inside me. They then ended up 'coming out sideways' in other behaviours instead. After a week of acting constantly happy, I broke down in floods of tears, overcome with deep feelings of grief. I then chided myself for 'failing' at manifesting. I hadn't yet learnt how to be kind to myself.

Suppressing our negative emotions is like putting a plaster over an infected wound. It may be temporarily hidden from view, but underneath the plaster it will become septic. We need to clean the wound first before we can allow it to heal.

This doesn't mean that we need to be perfectly healed before we can manifest anything. I have witnessed many spiritual people getting stuck in a perpetual cycle of never-ending healing. This comes from the belief that we need to be perfect to be able to be loved or get what we want in life.

I used to feel frustrated that I had spent so long on my healing journey and still hadn't got the results that I wanted. I saw getting into a happy relationship as a prize I would get at the end when I was healed and spiritual enough. This also led to me feeling resentment for others around me who I saw getting the things they wanted, even though they didn't seem to be working on themselves in the same way I was. Can you see what a lack mentality I was in?

Here's a news flash for you: the healing journey is never over. There are always new revelations, new discoveries and new layers. I'm grateful for this now because it makes life exciting. Now I'm excited when I get triggered because I know it's revealing something else in me to be healed, which will help me become even more of the person I want to be. Life is a process of letting go – gradually shedding layer after layer of everything that isn't love.

As you read the next section about techniques to release your limiting beliefs, please forget any idealised pictures of healing. Don't use your wounds as a stick to beat yourself with or a reason that you can't get what you want. Embrace yourself as the perfectly imperfect human you are. Remember, you deserve to be loved at every stage of your journey, wherever you are at.

Keep giving yourself love, being on your own side and treating yourself with huge amounts of compassion. If you can be there for yourself, you will attract people who can be there for you too. Identifying anything that is holding you back is another way of knowing, loving and supporting yourself.

## LET THE OLD MAN DIE

I've already mentioned some of the ways we can start to let go of our limiting stories but, in this chapter, I'll delve into this more deeply and tell you the exact techniques and practices that have worked for me.

Our 'old men' or negative beliefs can take several forms. They can be about ourselves, about a specific person (such as an ex or somebody we're attracted to), about a particular gender or about dating and relationships in general.

If you want to bring love into your life, you need to examine all these areas and get to the bottom of any old stories you need to release. Unfortunately, I held negative beliefs in all these areas: I believed myself to be unloveable, men to be unfaithful players, and dating and relationships to be hard. Was it any wonder that, while feeling so cynical, I struggled to believe that I would ever find the right person?

When you judge yourself, criticise yourself or are hard on yourself, you're dwelling at a lower frequency and will attract a relationship that reflects this back to you. Before you can have the love you want, you must believe in it energetically first.

# EMBODIMENT: EXAMINE
# YOUR LOVE STORY

Take this opportunity to take stock of your own stories. We're going to create a list which will show you what you're working with and what you need to let go of.

Complete the following sentences as many times as possible. Dig deep and keep going until you get to the underlying beliefs.

This may be hard, emotional or painful, so give yourself plenty of time, space and self-care as you complete this embodiment exercise. Be prepared to cry and release emotions if necessary.

> I believe men/women/people (whoever you are romantically interested in) are…
> When it comes to love, I believe I am…
> My past relationships have failed because…
> Relationships are…
> Dating is…
> My ex/last partner is…
> It's hard to find love because…

Now that you have your list of beliefs, I'm going to teach you some basic mindfulness techniques to change your story.

#TotallyLoveable @mindfuldivas

# TECHNIQUE ONE: IDENTIFY SECONDARY SUFFERING

All of us will go through pain, but suffering is optional. In other words, it's not what happens to us but the way we interpret and react to it that causes us the most problems.

A simple example would be if two people were stuck in a traffic jam. The person in one car spends the whole time getting angry, blaming other drivers, swearing and worrying about being late for their appointment. Meanwhile, the person in the second car decides there's nothing they can do about the situation, so they take a few deep breaths and use the extra time to listen to an audiobook.

Now both situations may have had the same outcome (being late for work), but which driver do you think suffered more?

Railing against something we can do nothing about doesn't help us and often makes us feel worse. The situation (being stuck in a traffic jam) is the primary experience, but when we resist the situation by imagining negative outcomes (like we're going to get in trouble at work) we add a layer of secondary suffering. In Buddhism, this is known as the 'second arrow'. Life shoots us with the first arrow (primary suffering), but we choose to stick the second arrow (secondary suffering) into ourselves, which make our pain worse.

How does this relate to dating? Take a few moments to imagine this scenario: you go on a great first date with a man. At the end of the evening, he kisses you goodnight and you go to bed feeling optimistic and excited. The next day you wait for his text, but it never comes. For the next few days, you're glued to your phone, desperate for a notification. Eventually, after a couple of days, you send him a message, but hear nothing back. You've been ghosted.

Now, what goes on in your body when you read this story? Firstly, you may notice the feeling of excitement – maybe the butterflies in your tummy or a light fizzy feeling in your body. Then, as you realised he wasn't going to text, what kind of feelings came up? Maybe you felt anxiety in your chest, a churning in your tummy, a tightness in your throat? Did you notice that you held your breath or didn't breathe as deeply? Maybe you felt feelings of sadness, anger and disappointment. This is your primary experience.

Next, notice what thoughts came up for you. Was this scenario familiar? If so, you may have experienced thoughts such as *this always happens to me, I shouldn't have got my hopes up, typical male dating behaviour* or *I've been rejected again, maybe I'll never find love.*

Maybe your mind starts to ruminate on the things you may have done wrong – wondering if your outfit wasn't right, you laughed too loudly, ate too much, weren't interesting enough, etc.

Any thoughts that come up for you which make you feel worse are secondary suffering you're adding to the situation. This is how we stab ourselves with the second arrow.

# EMBODIMENT: DON'T SHOOT
# THE SECOND ARROW

This is a mindfulness technique you can practise in everyday situations when things don't go your way or something difficult or uncomfortable happens. Once you've got used to the technique, you can eventually start to apply it to your dating life too.

Bring to mind a typical uncomfortable situation that may happen in everyday life. It could be something like getting stuck in traffic or being late for an appointment.

**Step one:** Identify your primary experience (this is what you can immediately feel with your physical senses and emotions).

**Step two:** Identify your secondary experience (the negative thoughts and beliefs you're adding to the experience).

**Step three:** Remind yourself that thoughts are not facts.

**Step four:** Return your attention to the primary experience and let yourself deeply feel your feelings without adding to the story. You can do this by tuning into the sensations in your body and focusing on the sensory experience.

Let me give you a simple example: imagine that you stub your toe. As well as feeling the pain, you blame yourself and call yourself stupid for not putting on slippers around the house or feel sorry for yourself, thinking it's an example of your bad luck. This is adding secondary suffering.

Instead, when you notice yourself thinking unkind or self-pitying thoughts, let them go and focus only on the physical sensation of the pain without adding guilt, self-hatred or blame.

The key here is accepting the situation as it is WITHOUT the extra layer of unhelpful thoughts. It's OK to feel our painful feelings (primary suffering), but we only make our situation worse when we add secondary suffering to them.

#TotallyLoveable @mindfuldivas

# EMBODIMENT: SECONDARY PAIN IN DATING/RELATIONSHIPS

Think back to a recent painful or uncomfortable situation in your dating life or relationship.

What was the situation?

**Step one:** Identify the primary sensations you experienced. These can be emotions such as anger, sadness and rejection, or physical feelings such as pain in your heart, stinging tears in your eyes, shortness of breath, a racing pulse, etc.

**Step two:** Identify any secondary suffering you added to the situation. This could be thoughts about yourself (e.g. I'm not good enough), thoughts about the other person (e.g. he's selfish) or thoughts about relationships in general (e.g. dating is a waste of time).

**Step three:** Tell yourself that thoughts are not facts and return to the primary experience. Lie down for a few moments with your hand on your heart and let your body feel any sensations arising. The idea is not to argue with the thoughts or try to think positive. It is simply to return to the experience of the body. This is mindfulness.

#TotallyLoveable @mindfuldivas

# TECHNIQUE TWO:
# JUMP OFF THE THOUGHT BUS

When we have ingrained habits of thinking certain thoughts, these translate into autopilot reactions. Like a muddy track trodden through a lawn, where people have walked over it, we create a shortcut in our mind. Every time we think the same outdated thoughts, the track gets more well-trodden, and it becomes harder to think in a different way.

This is a habit – just the same as reaching for the ice cream or wine when you've had a hard day or having a coffee in the morning.

We can even become addicted to our own negative habits of thought. For example, you may find your mind repeatedly wandering into thoughts that it's hard to meet someone, men don't treat you well, you're not good enough for love, or whatever your own story is. Even though you know these thoughts aren't doing you any good, it may feel hard to stop.

During the embodiment exercises in this book, you will have uncovered some of your habitual thought patterns. So, how can you deal with them when they come up in the moment? I'd like to share a mindfulness technique that you can use on a day-to-day basis whenever you find negative thoughts coming up.

Imagine your negative thoughts are a bus you take that leads you to a destination you don't want to go to – let's call it Negativity Town. Every day you wait at the bus stop and take the same bus. After a while, you take the journey on autopilot and are barely conscious of getting on the bus.

Now imagine that you don't want to get on that bus anymore. Instead, you're going to let that bus and any other buses to Negativity Town drive by. But you're so used to taking that bus that, if you don't pay close attention, you may find that you've jumped onto it automatically and are on your way to the wrong destination.

The key here is to stay very conscious and aware, so when you see the bus, you can make the deliberate decision not to get onto it. Because why would you want to get onto a bus that takes you somewhere you don't want to go? So, you stay still, breathe, focus on the sensations in your body and allow the bus to pass.

A great way to bring your attention back into the present experience is to focus on the feeling of your feet on the ground. Notice how your feet are feeling;

are they warm or cold? What is the texture of the ground or of your socks? Drawing our attention to the feet instantly drops awareness back into the body.

Another method is to focus on the temperature of the room. If you're outside, is there a breeze or is the sun on your face? The reason this works is because it is hard for our brain to focus on two things at once, so if we're fully present in the moment with our senses and physical body, it's difficult to be ruminating about the past or future at the same time.

Notice that we're not trying to argue against the thoughts or replace them with positive thoughts. We're just telling ourselves this thought is not relevant and helpful right now and it's much more useful to focus on the present moment.

This may seem hard at first, but the more you practise it, the more you will break the habit of jumping on the bus. Some days (in fact many, many times) you will realise that you're on that bus and on your way to Negativity Town. In those moments when you notice, don't beat yourself up or berate yourself that you've failed. It's quite the opposite – you've succeeded! You've noticed the fact that you're on the thought bus, when previously you may have sat on it for hours without being aware.

Give yourself a big pat on the back, congratulate yourself and very calmly get back off the bus. It doesn't matter how many times you have to do this; every single time is an amazing success.

The one thing that will really help you with this process is practising mindfulness meditation. This is different to the type of guided meditation where you listen to somebody's voice and are guided to relax or visualise. In mindfulness meditation, our aim is to stay awake and aware – paying attention to the breath and gently guiding our attention back to it every time our mind wanders.

Meditation of this type is sometimes known as concentration training because it trains our brain to be able to pay attention and to build new pathways, so we stop treading down that well-worn path on the lawn. The more you practise mindfulness meditation, the easier you will find it to control your thoughts in everyday life.

I suggest that you start by practising for at least 10 minutes a day and gradually build up to 20 minutes. If you don't already have a mediation practice, you can download a free breathing meditation from my website: themindfuldiva.com.

# TECHNIQUE THREE:
# FOR PERSISTENT THOUGHTS

If you find there are certain thoughts that come up for you repeatedly, no matter how many times you try to let the thought bus pass by, it's probably because these thoughts have a strong charge for you. Often these can be very deep unconscious beliefs that have been with you a long time – maybe since childhood.

Charged thoughts can include abandonment fears, fear of rejection and fear of getting hurt. These thought patterns are so pervasive because they have a strong emotion behind them –sometimes blocked feelings, which we couldn't express in the moment they occurred.

In mindfulness practice, rather than trying to eliminate, heal or get rid of our emotions, we bring acceptance to them. This may be a radical idea if you've been seeing your feelings as evidence that you're faulty or damaged. Instead of pushing away these feelings, we can choose to deliberately turn towards them with a huge amount of compassion and kindness.

Many of these emotions were formed when we were hurt as a child, so treat these young parts of yourself with the same tenderness as you would a child who fell over and hurt their knee or was upset because another child had been unkind to them.

By trying to let go of our negative thoughts (secondary suffering), we're not actually trying to get rid of or change our feelings. When something painful comes up, instead of engaging with the thought, try noticing what you can physically feel in your body.

Take time to lie down in a quiet place and give yourself space to feel whatever comes up. Pay attention to your breath, noticing the effect it has on your body. Now place your hand on the area where any pain is coming up for you. Commonly this may be the heart centre, the belly or the throat, but it could be somewhere else. Notice without judgement.

Feel the bodily sensations coming up without trying to resist or push them away. Keep breathing deeply and noticing the waves of sensation. If you feel numbness that's OK too – just keep noticing whatever is there.

Allow any tears to flow and any noises to come up that naturally arise, such as sighing, wailing, or moaning. Let whatever needs to be expressed by the body be expressed. Don't focus on the thoughts arising – stay out of your head and move into your body. Make sure to keep breathing as you feel into your emotions, rather than contracting and holding the breath.

Go very gently with this process and, if it ever becomes too intense or painful, stop and gently bring yourself back to the present moment by focusing on the colours, smells, sound and temperature in the room. The idea here is to gently lean into your feelings, not to force anything or subject yourself to extreme discomfort. You can always go back to the exercise another time when you're feeling stronger.

Keep reminding yourself it's OK to feel and give yourself compassion, kindness and love. You may need to repeat this embodiment exercise several times, whenever painful feelings arise.

If this feels too intense for you, you can try expressing your feelings through dance. Put on a sad, angry or moving song and really move to the music, letting your emotions be expressed through the body.

The key is to allow all your experience with acceptance and honour your feelings. We all feel pain and it doesn't mean you're broken – you just need to express it and let it out in a safe way.

It's possible that deep feelings from the past could arise during this exercise. If this ever feels unmanageable, please consult your GP and consider seeking professional help such as a trauma practitioner or counsellor.

## TECHNIQUE FOUR: EMOTIONAL FREEDOM TECHNIQUE

Emotional Freedom Technique (EFT) is a powerful way of releasing trapped emotions by tapping on meridian points in the body. I personally use this modality to help myself on a regular basis. There are lots of videos available for free online that can teach you the basics. I like Brad Yates as he has lots of short YouTube videos on different topics that you can easily fit into your daily routine. I also discovered a different technique called Faster EFT on YouTube. Experiment and see what works for you.

The basic premise of EFT is that you tap on different energy points in the body while repeating a phrase. This is set up like this:

"Even though *state problem* I still totally love and accept myself."

As you move around tapping the different points, you can slightly change the phrase to bring out different aspects of the blocked emotion or problem.

For example: "Even though my date didn't call me back I still totally love and accept myself."

I've used EFT for everything from fear of speaking in public to headaches. But it's also great for dealing with any issues to do with love, relationships and self-worth.

## TECHNIQUE FIVE: RAPID TRANSFORMATIONAL THERAPY

After I started practising meditation daily, I found myself becoming much calmer, more peaceful and contented. I was able to notice and let go of many negative beliefs and patterns of thought. However, when I took this out into the dating world, I was still easily triggered because of deep-seated beliefs formed in childhood and throughout my life. Although consciously I knew these beliefs about myself were not true, they still felt painful.

I decided to try Rapid Transformational Therapy (RTT) – a method devised by Marisa Peer, which combines hypnotherapy with cognitive behavioural therapy (CBT), neurolinguistic programming (NLP), psychotherapy and neuroscience. The sessions involve being regressed back into your past to discover events still affecting your current reality.

I must admit that I didn't find RTT sessions easy at all. They lasted two to three hours, in which I was put into a suggestable state and regressed back to situations in which I had formed negative beliefs about myself. Some of these were situations I was aware were affecting me, but it also uncovered some things I'd been unaware of.

During a typical RTT session, I would visit around three scenes from the past. Then based on what was uncovered and a questionnaire filled out earlier, the RTT practitioner would create a hypnosis recording. You then listen to this recording at least once a day for 21 days.

The effects are subtle at first and I didn't notice that things were changing. But eventually, the messages implanted in my subconscious during the hypnosis started to work and my beliefs about what was possible for me changed. By the time I'd had three 21-day courses of RTT focused on different limiting beliefs, I was in a happy relationship.

The subconscious mind is a powerful thing and once you've released the negative beliefs and stories you're holding onto, it becomes easier to naturally attract what you want. However, nothing is a quick fix solution and I recommend that if you try RTT, you do it in combination with mindfulness to stay present in your body and aware when you are creating secondary suffering. Combining all these modalities together can be a powerful way to blast away those old stories and let the old man die.

## SEXUAL HEALING

Most women I know have some degree of sexual trauma. According to the 2017 figures from the charity Rape Crisis, around 20% of woman and 6% of men in England and Wales have experienced some type of sexual assault since the age of 16. These are based only on the incidents reported.

Not all sexual trauma is created by assault. Every time you have sexual contact which you don't want it creates trauma in your body. This often happens during first sexual experiences before becoming fully aware of your boundaries, but it can also happen in long-term relationships. Eventually, this trauma can lead to becoming desensitised, unable to feel during sex or too scared to have sex at all.

After my divorce, my abandonment issues were so strong that any physical intimacy brought up fears of being left and hurt. I would be left feeling nauseous, unable to work or concentrate, sometimes even in physical pain that would leave me curled up in a ball. It was clear these strong feelings were not coming from the present experience, but old memories that linked sex with rejection and abandonment.

The effect of this was to make me avoid intimacy altogether. It wasn't worth the excruciating emotional pain afterwards. Sometimes I worried I'd never have sex again. To facilitate my own sexual healing journey, I went through counselling and processed a lot of emotions.

If you have suffered a sexual assault of any kind, please contact an organisation such as Rape Crisis in the UK or a similar helpline in your country.

## SACRAL CHAKRA CLEARING

Chakras are an ancient energy system originating from India which were first mentioned in the Vedas, ancient sacred texts of spiritual knowledge dating from 1500 to 1000 BC. The Sanskrit word chakra refers to spinning wheels of energy in the body.

Although there is debate about the total number of chakras, it's generally agreed there are seven main ones that align along the spine. If one of these chakras gets blocked it can trigger a physical or emotional imbalance.

The sacral chakra (or *Svadhisthana*) is in the lower abdomen area and is represented by the colour orange. It's the chakra responsible for creativity, joy, pleasure, and sexuality. This means that it can be where sexual trauma is stored.

When this chakra is open, we experience the manifestation of our desires, improved relationships, emotional stability, sensuality, vibrant sexuality, playfulness and joy de vivre. But when it is blocked, we can feel stifled and experience reproductive problems, low libido, emotional instability, sexual dysfunction, menstrual issues and kidney disorders.

There are many ways to clear this chakra, including positive affirmations about sexuality, dancing, wearing orange and specific yoga positions which focus on the chakra. You can also place orange-coloured crystals such a fire opal or carnelian on the lower stomach area while you meditate.

I once did a course to clear my sacral chakra, which included wearing an obsidian crystal secured under a sanitary towel in my knickers for a week. I suffered tummy cramps the whole week I wore it – it literally felt like the negative energy was draining into the crystal. That's one of the more bizarre things I did in pursuit of healing.

Another way some women clear out stagnant sexual energy is through using a jade egg. This is an egg-shaped crystal made for vaginal insertion. They are believed to be Chinese in origin although some researchers have said there is no evidence to support this. There are also other types of eggs (known as yoni eggs) made from crystals such as rose quartz and obsidian.

The practice of using jade eggs attracted controversy when Gwyneth Paltrow wrote about it on her blog Goop in 2017. The mainstream media pushed back and pointed out there was a lack of evidence base for any health claims about the eggs and even suggested they could be potentially harmful. Some articles took a mocking tone of looking down on women's sexuality and agency over their own bodies.

Obviously, I'm not a doctor and am not qualified to give you medical advice. I can only tell you anecdotally that using a jade egg has been a useful healing practice in my own life. If this is something you would like to try, then I suggest you do your own research into the subject and decide if it feels right for you. This is your body and your choice.

My teacher was Layla Martin who runs yoni egg courses online and has training videos available on her website. She advises very specific practices for sexual healing, using the jade egg to clear out energy from past lovers.

## EMBODIMENT: SACRAL CHAKRA AFFIRMATIONS

How do you want to feel in relation to sexuality, pleasure and joy? Create a set of affirmations which encompass what you would like to embody in this area of your life.

For example:

It's safe for me to express my sexuality.

I love experiencing pleasure.

I experience joy and pleasure every day.

I flow with the creativity and passion of life.

I feel vibrant, alive and pulsing with energy.

I enjoy loving, healthy, pleasurable relationships.

Regularly write down these affirmations in your journal and repeat them to help clear your sacral chakra and stay in alignment with your intentions.

#TotallyLoveable @mindfuldivas

## A NOTE ON TRAUMA

Practising mindfulness or doing inner work can sometimes bring us in touch with underlying traumas. These could be things we're already aware of, such as having suffered abuse, being in an accident or suffering a serious illness. But trauma also relates to socioeconomic issues. Underlying trauma is caused by oppression and discrimination suffered due to race, gender, ethnicity, or sexuality. As a mixed-race woman from a working-class background, this is something I can personally relate to.

Trauma may also be related to incidences long-forgotten, buried in the subconscious or from when we were pre-verbal. Some events that have affected us deeply may not even appear to be particularly significant but can still have caused trauma.

If you're feeling either distressed or extremely disassociated from your body in meditation or life in general, it could be a sign that trauma is arising for you. Please do not try to push through this experience or 'just be' with it. This is when listening to our bodies becomes very important – there is a difference between allowing ourselves to feel into a painful sensation and becoming overwhelmed by it.

If at any time during meditation you feel distressed, I recommend turning your attention to the outer world rather than focusing on your body and your inner experience. Keep your eyes open and observe the physical things around you in the room or focus on the temperature in the room or sounds around you. It can be good to have an object or memory which makes you feel safe – such as holding a special crystal, stroking a pet or listening to music which soothes you. Return to these resources any time you feel out of your comfort zone. This will help you become more grounded in your present experience rather than any traumatic past experiences that may be coming up.

Sometimes focusing on the breath can feel too intense and, in these incidences, I advise you to choose another focal point, such as your hands, feet or the sensation of the chair or bed supporting you.

If you feel trauma is arising for you, it's important to seek the help of a qualified medical professional or counsellor who can help you.

Because this topic is so important, I trained in trauma-sensitive mindfulness with David Treleaven, so that I can spot signs of trauma in people who join my courses and offer appropriate support. Unfortunately, many meditation teachers are not trained in trauma and advice to 'just be' with extremely painful and traumatic feelings can be damaging. If you wish to continue exploring mindfulness, I recommend working with a trauma-informed teacher, such as myself, who can give you one-to-one help and recommendations.

# CHAPTER FIVE

# EMBRACE THE DARK FEMININE

"I am a forest, and a night of dark trees:
but he who is not afraid of my darkness, will find
banks full of roses under my cypresses."
– Friedrich Nietzsche, *Thus Spoke Zarathustra*

As a teenager I read a popular dating book which advised that women should act unavailable and follow strict rules to attract a male partner. I tried the method on a couple of boyfriends, and they were hooked – in fact, one proposed to me within six months. This may seem like a success story, but it was a toxic, unhealthy relationship.

When we play games in dating, we attract people who are not right for us, because we don't truly believe that our authentic self is good enough to be loved in its raw, authentic state.

At the time, however, I thought this dating book had shown me the secret to attraction. This behaviour of 'playing hard to get' became so deeply ingrained in me over the years that it was second nature. I would never dream of being open about my feelings, calling or texting a man first or even replying to his texts straight away.

Not only that, but 20 years later, after my divorce, I found modern-day 'feminine energy' coaches were now preaching the exact same rigid dating rules I'd been following such as 'leaning back' and being passive to 'hook your man'.

## DATING WITHOUT STRATEGY

A few years after my divorce I discovered a dating coach who taught about being open and honest about your feelings. This was a revelation to me after years of playing manipulative games with the opposite sex.

I found the idea this coach was preaching about being vulnerable and transparent to be frankly quite terrifying. How could such guilelessness possibly work? I feared I would lose all my intrigue and mystery and be taken for granted and walked over by men.

Still, something about the course obviously appealed to me because I signed up. It was a radical new concept – the idea that I could be myself, act naturally, be honest and still be attractive.

Around the same time, I started dating a new man – someone I'd had a flirtation with for several months. I went full in with my new tools, deciding that I would be totally open with him about my feelings. Not only did I not wait to text him back (as my past dating bible had suggested), but I actively texted him, called him and asked him on dates.

The problem was that I hadn't done a lot of inner work or healing at this point and was deeply triggered if he didn't react in the way I wanted him to. I had attracted this relationship from my wounds rather than from a place of self-love and power. It soon became apparent that he was unable to give me what I wanted, as he was going through a difficult divorce and custody battle that took up all his energy and attention. I felt tired of coming second place and listening to his ongoing childcare dramas. I wanted to be his number one priority, but that clearly wasn't possible.

Eventually I told him that I couldn't date him anymore. It felt I was taking what scraps of attention he threw me while I waited for his divorce to be over. Despite having deep feelings for this man, I knew my worth and wanted more.

When that relationship ended, I remember swearing never to open my heart to love again. As far as I was concerned, the course I'd taken was a total failure. I'd followed the dating coach's advice and I'd ended up getting hurt.

I returned to my manipulative dating strategies and now not only did my heart have walls around it, but prison bars. I'd forgotten that truly opening your heart is about feeling unconditional love no matter what. If I'd really loved that man, I would have been able to feel compassion for his situation and stay in the vibration of love rather than feeling anger at him for not conforming to what I wanted.

The key is being able to give yourself the love that you want from another person, but I hadn't yet learnt that lesson.

What I longed for was a man to break into my closed-off heart, for him to want me so much that he would scale those walls or take a battering ram to them. If anyone really loved me then they would see past my fears and protections and make me feel safe, I reasoned. And when this didn't happen, I went back to my default wound of feeling unloveable and not good enough. I was firmly encased in my victim story and didn't want to get hurt ever again.

## SACRED ANGER

A few months after my break-up with divorcé, I decided to get back on the dating scene. On an impulse, I accepted a last-minute date with an attractive Spanish architect I'd been chatting with on an app. Usually I like men to plan dates in advance, but I was on the rebound and in need of some fun and distraction.

I met him in a pub on London's Embankment and he was as good looking in the flesh as in his photos. But minutes after we sat down with our drinks, he started running his hand up my leg and trying to kiss me. It was obvious that he'd taken our flirty texting as a sign that sex was guaranteed, and he wanted it as quickly and easily as possible. I'd come with a totally different expectation of a light-hearted date but not a hook-up.

He wasn't happy when I refused his advances. I don't remember our exact conversation, but it soon escalated into an argument. Things got so heated that we both stormed out of the bar and, less than an hour after arriving, I was back on the train home.

This man was obviously a total idiot, but somehow, I took the evening as an indicator that I was unloveable. On the train home, I felt so ashamed that I'd been viewed me as such low value. I began to cry – partially about how he'd treated me, but also because I was still hurting over the end of my relationship with the divorcé.

After arriving home, I began aimlessly trawling through YouTube looking for consolation, when a video popped up about knowing your worth. I have no idea what search term I'd entered, but it was one of those moments that was to take my life in yet another totally new direction.

The video was by a spiritual teacher known as SheRa Seven who preached that women should start realising how valuable they are. As far as she was concerned, the idea of love and romance was a social construct designed to trap women into accepting too little from men. That night I stayed up late binge-watching her videos and felt a change coming over me – my heart was hardening.

Now I know this is a strange thing to write about in a book about mindfulness and love, but this was about to be a life-changing step on my journey. After spending several years meditating, learning relationship skills and talking about feelings, I suddenly felt I had been too open, too vulnerable, and too soft.

I was angry at the men who had hurt me: the lecherous architect, my supposed twin flame, my divorcé lover, my ex-husband and so many others. At that moment, I passionately hated men and, instead of being all love and light about it, I embraced the feeling of sacred anger and allowed it to rise in me.

It was then that I began to embody the energy of the dark feminine.

## DIVINE FEMININE

In the Abrahamic religions, there is a lack of feminine deities. I was brought up in the UK, where the predominant religion is Christianity. Our primary archetypes for women are the virgin embodied by Mother Mary and the whore embodied by Eve and Mary Magdalene.

However, there are theories that the existence of the divine feminine has been hidden from history by our patriarchal society to control women. There is evidence that Mary Magdalene and Mother Mary were spiritual leaders themselves, who studied the feminine mysteries. This dates back to ancient Egypt when it is said that women were priestesses at the temples and mystery schools of the Goddess Isis.

Pre-Christianity in Pagan times, people worshipped the Goddess, the Earth and lived in tune with the cycles of nature. But Christianity saw widespread femicide with women being burnt as witches for following these beliefs.

Many people believe that our present-day era is the rising of the sacred or divine feminine when systems of patriarchy will crumble, and new energy will begin to rule the Earth. Certainly, within my own lifetime, I've seen women discover more about the divine feminine and I've felt called to this myself. More books and information are readily available about living in tune with our cyclical nature, Mary Magdalene, witchcraft, Goddesses, female sexuality and the feminine healing arts. Also, increasing numbers of women are taking power by becoming entrepreneurs and starting businesses – many of which are to help others. Seeing this really heartens and encourages me.

I feel it's important for women to get in touch with the divine feminine in whatever way feels good. Learning and reading stories of Goddesses, female deities and feminine mysteries is one way to do this. I can recommend the books *You are a Goddess* by Sophie Bashford and *Women Who Run with the Wolves* by Clarissa Pinkola Estés.

Personally, I've found that this information comes to me naturally without me having to seek it. For example, in 2017 I felt called to journey to Glastonbury after randomly seeing an angel themed bed and breakfast (B&B) while watching TV on the treadmill at the gym. I don't usually watch TV, so it was only because this show happened to be on in the gym that I saw it. A few weeks later I woke up to hear a strong voice tell me very clearly to go to Glastonbury. I immediately booked the accommodation I'd seen.

When I arrived, the woman who owned the B&B was running a weekend training on ancient Egypt, and I ended up attending and learning about the Isis and the feminine mystery schools. Maybe you're experiencing this kind of synchronicity right now during this book? The very fact that you are reading these words tells me that this is an important message for you.

Getting in touch with your divine feminine nature is another way to come home to yourself and be in your power. During the time I connected with my dark feminine side, I was drawn to the energy of Santa Muerte, the female saint worshipped in Mexico as Our Lady of the Holy Death. With her skeletal appearance she may appear a frightening figure, but I felt her energy protecting and looking out for me as I embodied this stage of my life.

At other times, I've been draw to Aphrodite, the Greek Goddess of love, Fortuna, the Roman Goddess of prosperity and Kali the Hindu Goddess of death, time and change. Whenever I work with a certain Goddess, I learn as much as I can about her and display her picture on my altar to help tune into her energy.

## NO MORE GOOD GIRL

Within us all, we have different archetypes. For a long time, I had lived in my light feminine – I was ethereal, spiritual, loving, nurturing and motherly. Other times I was in my masculine energy – striving to do, achieve, work and earn money. But I had neglected the dark side of myself and now finally she saw her opportunity and was coming out to play.

I was a good person. I cried at the news. I gave to charities. I tried to help the world. I was honest. If I accidentally walked out of the supermarket without paying for something, I went back in again to pay. I believed in treating people fairly and doing the right thing. I had a conscience.

But there was a repressed part of me that had always been present under the surface in the shadows of my fantasies. She was a seductress, she turned heads, she lived for her own pleasure, a femme fatale, a heart-breaker. She was devious and manipulative and used her sexual charms to get what she wanted out of life. Her red lipstick was a type of dark magic. She enticed and enchanted. She was feared, hated and awed. She was everything that society had demonised and that I had rejected in myself.

I felt her presence grow within me with overwhelming power. She looked at the men I had been with and declared them pathetic, she laughed at the pain I had gone through.

*"Darling, get yourself together,"* she said.

For my new role, I needed to look the part. I had always been the fresh-faced girl-next-door. Now I started to invest in expensive makeup, wearing fake eyelashes, getting long acrylic nails done every week and wearing a waist trainer. These were all things I had considered unnecessary or even distasteful before, but now I wanted to experience what it was like to be a woman who shamelessly displayed her sexuality. Instead of my usual floaty floral dresses, I started to dress in tight-fitting clothes always paired with high heels.

I joined a 'sugar dating' Facebook group for women, which shared how to use the feminine arts of beauty, make-up, etiquette and clothing to attract wealthy men. This may seem a lot of work, but I enjoyed it. I was putting my time, attention and energy on myself.

Sugar dating (or sugaring) is a mutually beneficial exchange in which men pay for the time and attention of attractive women. I began to regard men as nothing but a means to an end and this made me feel powerful. Rather than the love I had been seeking for so long, I now wanted to use men for whatever I could get from them. I realised that I'd been ignoring an advantage that could get me ahead in life and I began to wield my sexuality like a weapon.

One of the basic premises of the community I joined was that men are untrustworthy and incapable of being faithful. We vowed not to get emotionally attached to them at any cost.

Instead, we dated men who had money and were generous with it. Many of the women in this community had personally experienced ill treatment, betrayal and infidelity from men, which led them to this path.

Our low opinions of men were confirmed as many of the men looking for this type of relationship were being unfaithful to their wives, had children older than the women they were dating, lied about their age, and were generally dishonest.

In return, we lied about our names, our age, our jobs and pretty much everything else. We saw our own dishonesty as necessary protection – a way of fighting fire with fire. When I told the other women my story about going into the dating world innocently looking for love, they saw me much as a lamb being thrown into a pit of wolves. And honestly that was how I had felt much of the time. Now I felt I finally had control and was the one calling the shots.

During this time, I hardened my heart, not only to men but to the world in general. I became more self-centred and started putting my own family first. I stopped being a walkover and going out of my way to help others. Instead of communicating honestly, I manipulated others by saying whatever was most likely to get me my own way. It was as if I had been blind and could finally see, as I realised that this self-centred way was how many people were living their lives.

My previous openheartedness now seemed laughably gullible and naive. I looked at everything with fresh eyes. Relationships I'd previously admired, I now viewed with disdain. The women were exhausted, worn out from working too hard and not cared for or looked after. They were the ultimate cautionary tale.

In contrast, we aspired to live a pampered life in which our needs would be taken care of, which allowed us to pursue our interests without having to work at jobs we hated and suffer from burnout. Some of the women in the group had big-spending sugar daddies who bought them apartments, paid them monthly allowances, and took them on expensive shopping sprees and holidays around the world. But this was not prostitution – the idea was to get as much as possible from a man without getting sexual. Being in the presence of our feminine energy was enough. When men became too demanding, we simply ditched them without explanation. There were always plenty more.

During that year, I dined at many of the top restaurants in London, had the best seats at West End shows, drank cocktails and champagne in rooftop bars, had dresses, jewellery and perfume bought for me, and was frequently given gifts of money. My home was constantly full of flowers and boxes of chocolates. But I didn't so much as allow a man to kiss me.

I may have been a single mum in my 40s with two children, but I began to see that rather than the damaged goods I'd thought I was, I was inherently valuable to men. The lesson I learnt was to embrace all the sides of myself: both the light and the dark. When you practice this, you signal to the Universe that you love yourself unconditionally.

# EMBODIMENT: SHADOW DESIRE INVENTORY

If you've experienced rejection in the past, you may have questioned your worthiness to be loved. Have you ever over-given, accepted too little or felt like a potential partner didn't see your value?

In this list, I want you to write down everything you desire. Please take out any ideas based on social conditioning, what you think is realistic, or what you believe is morally right or ethical.

Get in touch with your dark feminine – the side of you that is self-centred, that can have anything she wants at the click of a finger. Forget what people would think of you and express your most outrageous, unobtainable, greedy and obscene desires. Don't censor or judge yourself – the more outlandish and unreasonable the better. What would you want if you had no rules?

You don't ever have to act on any of this – it is just a way of getting in touch with your deepest and most taboo longings.

For example:

- I want a man who worships the ground I walk on and adores me.

- I want to have several partners at once.

- I want to eat at the world's best restaurants.

- I want to be fanned and fed grapes like Cleopatra.

- I want to have a huge diamond engagement ring.

- I want to drive a Porsche.

- I want to go for regular spa days.

- I want to not have to work.

- I want to go for a professional manicure every week.

- I want to go on exotic holidays to five-star hotels.

- I want to have long bubble baths.

- I want someone else to clean my house.

- I want to buy all the dresses and pretty things I like without worrying about the money.

If you're reading this book, it's likely you're a kind, sensitive soul – possibly someone who identifies as an empath or lightworker. Notice what feelings come up for you when you read this list – is a part of you repulsed, guilty, angry, triggered, judgemental?

Pay attention to what's coming up for you. Maybe the things you value are much simpler – sunshine, fresh air, friendship. I get it! But dig deeper – is there a secret part of you that longs to be a diva, a femme fatal, a seductress? Is a part of you turned on?

It's taboo for women to have desires. We're deeply conditioned by stories of women who want too much – look what happened to Eve in the Garden of Eden when she bit that apple.

What would it be like for you to be a woman who put herself and her own needs first? Feel into that reality and feel the power of it.

#TotallyLoveable @mindfuldivas

## BE YOUR OWN SUGAR DADDY

You may not want to try sugaring, but I hope you know that you're worthy of whatever you want in life. Look at the list of desires you made in the last embodiment exercise and decide how you can give yourself those things.

For example, you may not be able to go on an all-expenses-paid shopping spree, but could you treat yourself to a new dress? You may not be able to go to luxury spas every week, but could you book a pampering facial? If money is short, could you even give yourself a spa day at home?

This exercise is as much about spending time and attention on yourself as it is money. You may not be able to give up your job and be totally looked after, but are there any steps you can take to make your job less stressful or to spend more time focusing on the things that really interest you? For example, hiring a cleaner once a week for your home or getting a babysitter so you can go out for a night.

Your list is a map to your desires. Be your own sugar daddy and make yourself number one priority in your life without guilt. You're worth it!

## THE RETURN TO LOVE

My time sugaring gave me a tantalising glimpse of the lifestyle I could have, but whenever men wanted to make our relationship physical, I would back away. As much as I tried to convince myself that I didn't need love or an emotional connection, there was still a buried part of me that yearned for it.

I knew the walls around my heart had grown almost impenetrably high and I longed for a man willing to break through my defences and see the sensitive woman behind the make-up and high heels. But my new life was constantly reinforcing the idea that all men wanted was arm candy. Dating had become like acting a role in a play. It seemed impossible that anyone could ever love the real, flawed me underneath the glamorous façade I'd created.

Whenever I wavered, I would remind myself that I was doing this to give my two daughters a better life. I felt so guilty for the hardships they had endured because of my divorce and financial difficulties. In some way, I felt like that by using men I was fighting back against the patriarchy for all women.

I may have taken an extreme route, but this was a deeply healing journey for me. Instead of feeling a victim of my emotions and the dating game, I felt empowered. And seeing that men were willing to pay just to have me in their company helped me realise my worth.

Despite this, my hard-hearted persona was not to last. My local yoga studio was running gong baths – a type of sound healing, which sends out healing vibrations from a gong while you lie relaxing. I started going regularly and two experiences there were to crack my heart wide open again.

During the first gong bath, an image of my ex-husband drifted into my mind. I'd never fully grieved the relationship because I knew the breakup was the right thing. But, as the sound of the gong reverberated through my body, memories of happy times with my husband came back to me. Tears came to my eyes as I remembered that things had not always been bad – I had loved and been loved. When the session ended, the gong player ended with a simple question: "Who are you now?"

I heard the answer from inside me: *someone who believes in love.*

The walls around my heart had melted like a block of ice. I knew it was time to end the sugaring, but now I felt vulnerable and exposed. The thought of going back to dating men I was attracted to and who had the capacity to hurt me was terrifying. I'd been indoctrinated over the last year to avoid opening my heart at all costs. After all I had been through, was I really willing to risk being hurt again?

It was at another gong bath that I got a message of hope that kept me going through that hard time.

As I lay down on the yoga mat feeling the deep vibrations of the gong pulsing through my body, memories of some of my deepest wounds and fears about being unloveable arose. This was deep stuff from my childhood and even ancestral wounds about my family lineage. I was on an internal journey seeing image after image of my failures, losses and shame. I'd quietly cried in gong baths before, but this time the tears flowed, and I hid my face under the blanket to hide the sobbing.

Eventually I heard a voice speak. It wasn't the guy playing the gong or anyone else in the room. This voice came from inside. But it wasn't my own thoughts – it was a spoken voice as clear and resounding as a preacher on a pulpit.

*"Life won't let you have anyone who isn't right for you. Stay on your true path and you will meet your soulmate. He will love you completely despite all the things you think are wrong with you and all your insecurities and pain. You'll tell it all to him and it won't change how he feels about you. He will only love you more."*

A feeling of being completely safe flooded over me as I was overcome by a warm sensation of peace and calm. There was no evidence this dream man existed and it seemed almost impossible to believe there could be someone like that out there for me. Yet, at a deep level, I recognised this message as the truth. Now I had clear instructions – all I had to do was to stay on my path.

After the gong bath, I wrote the words into the notes on my iPhone, so I could remember them. Many times, over the next year when I was close to losing hope, I reread those words. Did they come from my higher self, the Universe or the spirit of the gong? I'll never know, but they were exactly what I needed to hear to keep my heart strong on my quest for love.

# CHAPTER SIX

## GET VULNERABLE AF

"To love someone fiercely, to believe in something
with your whole heart, to celebrate a fleeting moment in
time, to fully engage in a life that doesn't come with
guarantees – these are risks that involve vulnerability
and often pain. But I'm learning that recognising and
leaning into the discomfort of vulnerability teaches us
how to live with joy, gratitude, and grace."
– Brené Brown, *The Gifts of Imperfection*

Fear tries to keep us safe. That's why some women
pay thousands to expensive dating coaches or read
books telling them to follow a rigid set of rules to
attract a man.

We want someone to tell us the answer because we're scared of getting hurt and we try to defend ourselves with strategies like not texting back, pretending to be elusive or not showing our true feelings.

I know this because I've tried it all. Sorry to break this to you, but there is no guaranteed formula for love. Showing your true self feels vulnerable AF!

When you come from a place of fear and trying to protect yourself, you're in the wrong vibration for love. After giving up the sugaring, I was still struggling to open my heart.

It was around this time that I was made redundant from my job as a business reporter and decided to train as a mindfulness teacher. Dating became less of a priority, as I immersed myself deeply into self-discovery and meditation. Over months of training, I became more loving and connected to myself than I'd ever been before. I was finally stepping into my soul's purpose.

One day, randomly on Facebook an advert popped up for a tantric speed dating event. My curiosity was piqued, but I was nervous. Privately I had dabbled with tantra and had taken an online course on using a jade egg to heal from sexual trauma. But, despite all the work I'd done alone, I hadn't felt brave enough to connect in real life with any tantric men.

I'd seen 'conscious dating' events advertised before but had lacked the confidence to go – partially for fear that they'd be full of lecherous men with wandering hands. But somehow, despite my apprehension, this time I felt strongly called to go to the tantric speed dating event. Little did I know that I was about to have an experience which would finally break the walls of my heart wide open and allow it to heal.

Knocking at the door of a yoga studio near London's Victoria Station, I wondered what on Earth I was letting myself in for. Would the night involve physical contact with creepy men, nudity or embarrassingly awkward exercises? To make things worse, I'd arrived late and had to walk red-faced and flustered into the room when the event had already started.

Despite the teacher's instruction to remain non-judgemental, I instinctively cast a glance around the room to ascertain the attractiveness of the men. My eyes were instantly drawn to a South Asian man opposite me, whose energy was so radiant, he almost seemed to glow. I felt excited about the prospect of doing a tantric exercise with him.

Unlike traditional speed dating, there was no small talk – instead, the men stood around in a circle as the women moved around the room taking part in short exercises with each partner, designed to create connection. These interactions could involve touch, gazing into each other's eyes or simply being present with one another.

For one of the exercises, the teacher invited us to hug the person we were working with – who for me in this case was a tall, smiley Italian man. Although he looked friendly, it wasn't easy for me to be so intimate with a stranger and I felt self-conscious.

"Can we hug just a little?" I asked the Italian shyly.

He encouraged me to do whatever I was comfortable with, so I lay my head tentatively on his shoulder with his arms around my waist. I felt myself relaxing into the moment, as he held me tenderly without demands or pressure.

The last man I had dated had become physically pushy on our second date, trying repeatedly to get me to stay at his place despite me saying that I wasn't ready. The experience had left me feeling wary and disappointed in dating once again. I'd felt like sex was the only thing men wanted me for, but now here

I was with this man's arms around me with absolutely no expectations.

Women were guided by the teacher to remember a time in our past when we needed male support. As we mentally relived this experience, the male partners offered us loving words.

The tall Italian whispered in my ear: "I apologise on behalf of all the times my brothers have hurt you."

I felt his words permeate my body and my heart. Although he was a stranger, hearing these words as he held me in his arms was deeply healing. By the time the exercise ended, I was in a sleepy state, feeling supported, peaceful, grateful and open. Something inside me had shifted permanently.

At the end of the night, the glowing Asian man invited me to join him for a drink at a local bar and we continued to date for several months until he moved to the USA for work.

My heart finally began to open again. It was no coincidence that not long afterwards I started dating a Swedish man, who was to become very important in my life.

# EMBODIMENT: REMEMBER
# WHEN YOU NEEDED LOVE

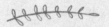

You can repeat this tantric exercise by yourself, using the power of your mind. Lie down and close your eyes. Imagine yourself being held by a masculine presence, which loves you deeply and unconditionally with no demands.

Once you've established this feeling, send yourself back in your imagination to a time in your life when you were hurt by a man. Open your heart and let any feelings, tears or anger naturally arise.

As you get in touch with this memory, imagine the spirit of the masculine whispering apologies to you as he holds you in his arms. Allow yourself to be supported throughout this experience.

When you have finished this embodiment exercise, take time to integrate slowly into your daily life, as a deep healing will have taken place. Drink some water, journal about your experience, and go slowly and gently about the rest of your day.

This exercise can also be repeated, remembering a time you were hurt by a woman and imagining being held by the spirit of the feminine.

#TotallyLoveable @mindfuldivas

# OPEN YOUR HEART TO LOVE

In order to attract the love you want, you have to let go of everything that doesn't serve you anymore, so you can step into the full power and strength of your beautiful, worthy and *Totally Loveable* self.

If you've been hurt before, it's not easy to open your heart again. When we've been let down by past relationships, we expect it to happen again and create an energetic block to love. Sometimes we may not even be aware that our heart is closed.

Opening your heart means:

- Not blindly following dating guidance (you know those YouTube videos or Facebook ads that pop up telling you how to become irresistible to a man or how to text a woman in a way that makes her beg for you? No, just no!)

- Not operating from strategies or techniques aimed at protecting yourself from getting hurt or making yourself seem more attractive.

- Being radically honest about who you are and what you want from a relationship.

- Not trying to hide the parts of yourself that you think are unloveable or unacceptable.

- Being open, even when it makes you feel like a total idiot and you're going to die of humiliation.

- Believing in the truth of love, even when there's no evidence.

- Keeping your heart open, even when you've been rejected, you feel like there's nobody out there or you don't believe anyone can love you for who you are without strategies and games.

In her book, *Light is the New Black*, Rebecca Campbell talks about the peony – a flower that opens wide and, when it seems like it can't open any more, it still somehow opens further. Be like that flower and open again and again and again.

*When it hurts, stay open anyway.*

*When it feels excruciating, stay open anyway.*

*When you want to run away, stay open anyway.*

*When you feel like hiding, stay open anyway.*

*Open, open, open, open.*

# EMBODIMENT:
# HEART-OPENING RITUAL

Create yourself a beautiful love ritual. Firstly, gather your materials: rose petals, rose oil and rose quartz crystals. Light a candle and run yourself a bath, adding a few drops of rose oil, a few rose petals and the crystals. You may also want to add Epsom salt, sea salt or other bath salts. Soak in the bath for at least 20 minutes.

When you leave your bath, wrap yourself in a warm towel and cover your body with lotion, really taking time to massage and give your love to every part of you. While you do this, listen to music that you find relaxing or uplifting. Repeat to yourself the mantra, "I am loved, I am loveable, I am love."

This is a lovely ritual to do before going to bed. The more you repeat this, the more you will feel your self-love grow.

#TotallyLoveable @mindfuldivas

# OPEN YOUR HEART CHAKRA

My first heart chakra opening was in 2014, after I'd been meditating regularly for around a year. At the time, I was taking a course titled 'Who hates the Metta Bhavana?' at the London Buddhist Centre.

Metta Bhavana is the loving kindness meditation I learnt on my first retreat at Taraloka. It involves focusing *metta* (the Pali word for loving kindness) in turn towards yourself, someone you like, someone neutral, someone you have a difficult relationship with and to all sentient beings. The course was about the blocks that come up when we try to do this.

Some people on the course struggled to feel *metta* towards the difficult person, some with sending *metta* out into the world, many struggled most with focusing *metta* on themselves. One thing was clear: feeling loving kindness isn't easy and we explored our resistance to every facet of the practice.

At this time, I started to experience an almost painful level of openness in my heart. It was like the walls I had carefully constructed over years began to melt away, leaving my heart soft and defenceless. I began to cry at the slightest thing, feel deeply sensitive to others' feelings and see beauty and tenderness everywhere.

I was not the only one feeling this way; in the question time at the end of each class, other participants confessed that they had become profoundly sensitive. One man said that he couldn't stop crying every day.

Unfortunately, in our fast-paced world, it's difficult to function with this level of openness, which is probably why we learn to harden our hearts to survive. This is especially relevant to men, whose assigned role in society is to be the strong ones who are prepared to go out to war for their country. Patriarchal, capitalist society needs us to close our hearts so we can be productive workers and soldiers. We may not even be aware to what extent our hearts our closed. However, by repeating heart-opening meditations regularly, we can undo some of this damage.

# EMBODIMENT: METTA BHAVANA MEDITATION

After reading about my experience with the Metta Bhavana, you may feel curious to try this loving kindness meditation for yourself. This is a meditation based on the *Metta Sutta*, the Buddha's words on loving kindness.

You may not feel much at first when you practice this meditation, so don't be discouraged if you're not able to get in touch with feelings of love or kindness. It may even feel awkward, inauthentic or bring up feelings such as anger or sadness.

Simply observe whatever comes up for you with self-compassion. Any negative feelings you experience are simply part of the process of letting go of everything that isn't love. As you continue to practice this meditation daily, you will experience your heart opening more and more.

Settle into a meditative posture and bring your attention to your breathing. Close your eyes if that feels comfortable or keep them downcast to reduce external stimuli.

Once you've settled and are feeling relaxed, bring to mind someone you care about. It could be a good friend, loved one or a pet. Choose someone it is easy for you to get in touch with your positive feelings for. Feel the sensation of love in your heart centre. You may feel it like a warmth in your body. You could even imagine it as colour or light emanating out from your heart. Offer this loved one a few phrases of loving kindness:

> *May you be well.*
>
> *May you be happy.*
>
> *May you be free from suffering.*
>
> *May you be loved.*

Now imagine sending this loving kindness to yourself, feeling that colour or light radiating through your body. Say to yourself the phrases:

> *May I be well.*
>
> *May I be happy.*
>
> *May I be free from suffering.*
>
> *May I be loved.*

Next think of a neutral person – somebody in your life you know but have no strong feelings for. For example, it could be somebody who works in a shop you go to regularly or a neighbour you don't know very well. Get in touch with a sense of well-wishing for this person and offer them the phrases:

> *May you be well.*
>
> *May you be happy.*

*May you be free from suffering.*

*May you be loved.*

Next imagine somebody you find difficult. It is not recommended to go for anyone who has abused or deeply hurt you. Instead, start by choosing somebody that you feel mildly irritated by. You may find it hard to get in touch with your feelings of well-wishing for this person. If so, remain in touch with your intention to send them kindness, even if you can't feel it. Again, offer the phrases:

*May you be well.*

*May you be happy.*

*May you be free from suffering.*

*May you be loved.*

Now, imagine your loving kindness radiating out from your body and into the room and building, spreading to anyone else in the vicinity. Then feel it radiating out into your road, your town, your country, your continent and eventually the whole world. Imagine yourself sending out this loving kindness to all beings.

Finally, let go of any effort, return to the sensation of the breath in the body. When you're ready, gently open your eyes.

#TotallyLoveable @mindfuldivas

# BREAK THE RELATIONSHIP RULES

You'll find all sorts of rules and judgements in the dating world – especially if you follow relationship coaches, watch YouTube videos and join Facebook groups. Everyone has an opinion on how to find love. Some experts say you should wait three dates to sleep with a man, some say three months, some say not until you're engaged. There are differing rules about how quickly to text back, how keen to act, what to say, how to dress, whether to split the bill 50/50 or let him pay.

If you try to follow all these rules, you'll end up driving yourself insane. Have you ever wondered how the whole of humanity has managed to perpetuate itself for thousands of years without a rule book? I bet if you look at many of your happily married friends, most of them didn't need a love coach to tell them what to do.

The truth is that the only way to attract the person who's right for you is to be yourself. Because if you're pretending to be someone else then how the hell is the right person going to recognise the magnificent weirdo that you are?

My boyfriend and I love being geeky, talking about our guinea pigs and lots of other oddball things. By the time I started dating him I'd pretty much given up trying to hide my real self – and I think that was the best thing I ever did. Because the reason I'd hidden myself in the past was because I feared that if a man really knew me, he would judge me as not good enough.

Having a partner who sees the real you – even when you're being insecure or emotional – means that you know they love you for who you truly are, and that's a good feeling.

When you pretend to be something you're not, you attract wounded people, who are scared to commit and love the thrill of the chase. This leads all too often to situations in which one partner pursues while the other is in some way unavailable. I believe these push/pull situations come from a deep fear of being really seen and known, often caused by not having healed from past hurts.

The only way to find love is the scariest, most vulnerable thing of all – letting your true self shine through.

# EMBODIMENT: THE TRUE YOU

Make a list of all the things that you try to hide from a date or new romantic partner. Maybe there are things about you that you think are unattractive, embarrassing, 'too much' or just plain weird.

For example, do you try to hide:

- Parts of your body you don't like or physical scars,

- your quirky sense of humour,

- your unusual taste in movies/music/food,

- your spiritual side?

One of the things that I always dreaded disclosing to my dates was that I'm both vegan and gluten-free. I feared they would be put off and assume I was a fussy nightmare to eat out with. But my current partner admires my ethics and has even started eating vegan too.

There's never anything about you that's wrong. When you find the right person, they will love everything about you, even the parts you don't like about yourself. Hold out for that person and keep being you no matter what.

#TotallyLoveable @mindfuldivas

# MASCULINE/FEMININE ENERGY

Within the world of dating and relationship experts, there is a lot of emphasis on women staying in their feminine energy to attract a masculine counterpart through polarity. This is the idea that opposites attract. Rather like the yin yang symbol, a relationship requires two different energies to feel alive.

The masculine or yang side is associated with qualities such as doing, achieving, leadership, directing, pursuing, analysing and discipline, whereas the feminine or yin side is associated with being, yielding, receptivity, softness, flowing, mystery and presence.

Because we live in a patriarchal society, both men and women typically need masculine characteristics to be successful in the workplace. A woman may be very successful in her career, used to calling the shots, leading others and achieving, but if she takes this energy into her romantic life, it will force her partner into taking more of a feminine role.

This is when you see women 'chasing' men, organising dates and directing the relationship, resulting in the men becoming passive and not feeling inspired to take the lead. Women are often encouraged by dating coaches to 'lean back' by not reaching out first to men, allowing the male partner to initiate contact and arrange dates.

While it's important that women embody their feminine energy, I have a slightly different take on this dynamic. As I mentioned in a previous chapter, I followed dating advice like this for many years. I would never text or call a man first, arrange (or even suggest) a date, compliment a man or do anything else to take the lead. However, I was repeatedly disappointed that this didn't work. A coach's response would be that this was because the man wasn't 'masculine' enough or was not interested enough (remember the book and movie *He's Just Not That Into You*). However, when this leaning back tactic failed again and again, I began to question it.

The truth is much more nuanced than that one partner must embody the masculine and the other the feminine. What I find in my relationship is that my partner has encouraged me to move more into my healthy masculine energy by helping me to implement more systems in my work, become more grounded, productive and organised. I feel confident to book or arrange things that I would like us to do as a couple, to call or text him when I want to and to give him compliments about his looks and qualities.

All these things are discouraged by certain relationship experts.

I've also encouraged him to get more in touch with his healthy feminine side by practising mindfulness and getting in touch with his emotions. It feels like we complement each other perfectly and to achieve this I don't have to stay 100% in feminine energy – I can embody all the sides of myself, and he can embody all the sides of himself. In fact, we nurture and tend to all the sides of each other.

Primarily, he has more masculine energy and I have more feminine, so in this way our dynamic feels very balanced. However, this isn't due to me acting a certain way or deliberately adopting any set of characteristics – I just allow my natural feminine nature to shine through. In this way, it doesn't matter if I call him 100 times a day – he still experiences me as a feminine woman.

It's not your actions that count so much as the energy behind them. If you're secure in yourself, you can be the one to text first and it doesn't matter, but if you're insecure all the leaning back and playing hard to get in the world won't help. Your authentic energy and sense of worthiness will always be felt.

The key to this is being true to yourself and letting your spirit shine through. This means dropping whatever fear-based behaviours and defences you have up to protect yourself, control the situation or try to manipulate. Balance comes from accepting, nurturing and loving all the sides of yourself and your partner or the people you date. This allows you to experience being in both feminine and masculine energies at different times, but not becoming too deeply entrenched in either one.

## EMBODIMENT: MEET YOUR INNER FEMININE AND MASCULINE

Close your eyes if it's comfortable for you, take a few deep breaths and get into a meditative state. Maybe place your hand on your heart if that feels good. Begin to imagine your inner feminine. If you're a visual person, you may be able to see her clearly, or if you may simply sense her energy.

What does she look like?

How does she move?

What does she love to do?

What message does she have for you?

How can you support her more?

What do you feel towards her?

Does she remind you of anybody? Notice what comes up.

Gently let her go and begin to feel into your inner masculine.

What does he look like?

How does he move?

What does he love to do?

What message does he have for you?

How can you support him more?

What do you feel towards him?

Does he remind you of anybody?

Gently let him go and, when you feel ready, open your eyes and bring yourself back to the present moment.

Journal about what came up for you in the meditation. Are there any messages that your inner feminine and masculine had for you? What actions can you take to support them more? Write about how you can find more balance between your masculine and feminine sides.

If nothing comes up for you, that is OK. Be alert to messages and revelations over the coming days as your subconscious continues to work on this issue.

#TotallyLoveable @mindfuldivas

# CHAPTER SEVEN

# FORGIVE THE MASCULINE

"As above; so below. As within; so without. As with the
universe; so with the soul."
– Hermes Trismegistus

Being a woman can sometimes feel scary. We're
taught from a young age that we must be careful of
where we go, what we wear and who we talk to. Mur-
ders and violence against women are in the news
every day. As I write this book, a young woman called
Sarah Everard has been murdered in the UK and a
movement called *Reclaim These Streets* is campaigning
for an end to violence against women.

Male violence against woman is the reason we're
taught our skirts mustn't be too short or our tops too

low. It's the reason we learn we shouldn't go out alone at night and need to be on constant alert. The reason we must walk quickly and purposely, avoiding dark alleyways and clutching our keys in our hands ready to gouge out the eyes of anyone who attacks us.

Stories on the news are terrifyingly unfathomable: men killing their wives and their children because of jealousy, rape of children and babies, child pornography, sex trafficking, abuse of women in the workplace. We learn we must be aware. Never relax. Stay alert. This was the deep wound I carried, which stopped me from trusting men.

Two years after I'd closed my heart to the possibility of love, I decided to try trusting men again. After the experience at the tantric dating event, I began to open my heart. It was the most vulnerable I'd let myself be for many years. I had been so stuck in the mentality of sugaring without emotion that spending time with men I found attractive seemed unnecessarily risky. Now I dipped my toes cautiously back into the water of my desires.

It was a slow process of allowing my nervous system to calm down and accept that being with a man I liked didn't always have to mean danger. I found myself unable to sleep in bed beside a man. Dating sent me into fight or flight mode. I was triggered by texts, or by the lack of texts. I worried about doing or saying the wrong thing.

Although I was trying to have loving relationships, I didn't truly believe that a man could love me. I saw men as incapable of tenderness or fidelity and still carried an innate fear of the masculine. My beliefs manifested and things fizzled out with everyone I dated– including the Swedish guy.

## THE ORGASMIC LIFE

Things changed during lockdown when I discovered orgasmic meditation or OM. I know this practice sounds weird – and maybe it is – but I was led to it in extraordinary ways.

The first time I heard about OM, I was attending a women's circle at which the facilitator mentioned she was an orgasmic meditation trainer. I didn't know what she was talking about, so didn't pay much attention.

Coincidentally a few months later, I went on a date with a guy who mentioned he had practised OM and explained what it was. I'm sure you're also feeling curious so let me explain: OM is a partnered meditation practice in which one partner strokes the other's clitoris for 15 minutes with no goal other than to feel.

OM is not foreplay or even considered sexual but is rather a deep mindfulness practice with many emotional and spiritual benefits. By allowing yourself to stay present to the sensations in your body you increase your ability to hold intensity, discover what turns you on and express your desires. To learn more, I recommend the book *Slow Sex: the art and craft of the female orgasm* by Nicole Daedone.

My date told me about a lesbian who turned up at his house to practice OM. After stroking her for 15 minutes, she climaxed and left, leaving him feeling used. I couldn't help but smile at how the tables had been turned on the usual story of men using women for sexual fulfilment.

After that, I started hearing about OM everywhere I went. It turned out that a tantra teacher I was working with had been involved in the scene, I dated another man who had tried it and even two random self-help books I read mentioned it. The Universe was clearly trying to give me a message.

Now, as you know, I have a rule to act on anything I hear about three times, but in this case it didn't seem possible. OM had been started by a company called OneTaste that had dissolved a few years earlier after facing various controversies. It seemed like my chance to try OM was gone. But yet again it seemed the Universe had other ideas.

I met a man at an online tantric event, and we instantly connected. Amazingly, it turned out that he also practised OM and he put me in touch with a female OM coach who could train me online. I had to invest some money, but I wasn't doing it for him. Somehow, I knew this was the next step on my path and it was going to hold something revolutionary for me.

## IN AT THE DEEP END

I decided to throw myself in without reservation to my relationship with the new man I'd met online. It was lockdown and we were having long Zoom calls every night in which I bared my soul. So many times, I'd held back and still ended up getting hurt, so what did I have to lose? We had lots of deep conversations and he shared with me some of the pain men experienced in being demonised by women and society. For the first time I started to consider things from the male point of view.

As well as connecting with the divine feminine, I now began to reconnect with the energy of the sacred masculine, embodied by figures such as Jesus, Shiva, Buddha, and the Green Man. I was gradually becoming receptive to loving and trusting the masculine. A lot of the masculine energy we see in the world is wounded and toxic, but the sacred masculine also needs to be nurtured to bring balance to the world.

One day, as I pulled an oracle card from Rebecca Campbell's *Work Your Light* deck, I had a startling revelation.

'Break the Chain' was the title of the card and it read: 'What old ways of being from your family line are you ready to let go of?'

I realised the wounds I was carrying were not only my own – they came from my relatives, ancestors and all the women who had ever lived. In my heart, I knew I needed to let go of this hatred and fear of the masculine that had been part of my life for so long. I didn't want this pain, fear and shame to be handed down to my daughters and the first step was to eliminate it from my own reality. Healing the world had to start with healing myself.

Rather than berating men, I had to take responsibility for being the change I wanted to see in the world (as Gandhi famously said). Even though I longed for a world in which people treated each other with compassion, I hadn't been able to express compassion towards men because of my fear of being hurt, abused or humiliated. Keeping walls up around my heart felt like protection, safety, prudence, common sense and wisdom – as obvious as putting a lock on your front door to prevent a burglary. But now I saw that these walls had to come down.

A part of me desperately wanted to keep safe and continue to barricade my heart. I felt a raw exposed terror – a fear of total annihilation. But how could I expect the world to open to love if I couldn't do it myself? How could I object to misogynists who hated women, when I was wracked with pain, hatred and resentment towards men? I decided I would have to crack open my heart, regardless of how much it hurt. Even if it destroyed me. I had to live in alignment with my belief in love.

A few years earlier, I'd undergone a past life regression, a gentle form of hypnosis in which I was taken back through time to my previous incarnations on this planet. In a trance state, I had seen my life as a gypsy called Angela living in Italy who danced in a travelling circus for a living. Although I loved the freedom of dancing, my husband was abusive and demanding. Life was cruel and hard, and I eventually died through suicide.

In another past life, I'd lived in a tiny cottage where I grew herbs in my garden to sell to neighbours who came to me for healing. But after my sister betrayed me for being a witch, I was put into stocks to be humiliated by the villagers before being banished to the woods, where I eventually died alone in the cold. Whether these past lives truly happened or reflected something within my subconscious didn't matter. Either way, they needed healing.

As well as the trauma, abandonment, and suppression of my feminine energy in my past lives, I could feel the burdens of my ancestral line in this lifetime, the heaviness of the past – the pain, the rejection, the lack of love my relatives had suffered throughout time. I felt deeply connected to my African female ancestors who had been treated as possessions, raped and dehumanised. I carried this terrible pain in my cells and my DNA.

At that moment, standing on the precipice of taking what felt like a huge risk to trust again, my mission on Earth became clear. I was here to share the message of forgiveness, kindness, compassion, understanding and love with other women who had been hurt. These were all qualities that not long ago I had rejected and turned my nose up at, believing they would make me weak. But now I was coming from a true place of power.

I was determined to bring love to those who needed it – those men I could see were broken and hurt. Even if it meant I must sacrifice my self-protection and risk being wounded again. I would stand for love even when it hurt.

Finally, it felt like I was living for something so much bigger than myself, and I birthed a new purpose, a new reality and the possibility of a new Earth. By activating this energy in myself, I activated it in others too.

# EMBODIMENT: WHAT DO YOU HAVE ON MEN?

Look inside you to discover what beliefs and fears you have about men. If, deep down, you hold negative beliefs about the opposite sex, you won't ever truly connect to them. Your subconscious will try to protect you by preventing you from getting too close. This exercise can also be carried out for women.

Finish this sentence as many times as you can and see what comes up for you:

Men are…

For example:

Men are unreliable.

Men are scared of commitment.

Men are unpredictable.

Men are violent.

Men are unfaithful.

Men are losers.

Men are scary.

Keep going until you run out of things to say. You can repeat this embodiment exercise any time you're triggered or feel fears about men coming up.

This is based on an exercise called spring cleaning from the book *Mama Gena's School of Womanly Arts*. I practised this with a friend over text messages for several years and we would take it in turn to ask each other the question: "What do you have on men?"

When the other person responded with their list, we would reply, "Thank you," and then swap over.

This was great for letting go of any negative beliefs I was holding or any pain coming up for me. We did this in writing, but you could also do this exercise verbally with a friend or study buddy.

#TotallyLoveable @mindfuldivas

## THE BREAKING OPEN

The decision to trust men again was huge for me. It felt akin to displaying a precious piece of jewellery unattended in a public place and believing it wouldn't be stolen. It wasn't just a mental decision; I felt a palpable difference in my energy.

At first, I experienced a gorgeous sense of freedom and happiness at my choice to spread more love in the world. But soon I found myself once again thrown into the depths of body-shuddering pain as my heart cracked open. The traumas I thought had healed once again returned. My chest physically ached as I remembered the agony of abandonment and rejection I'd faced in the past.

As lockdown lifted, I moved from meeting my date on Zoom to in person. It was around then I noticed red flags. In real life he wasn't the same as he'd seemed online. Had he tricked me into believing he was a deep and sensitive man? I couldn't tell if I had been too open, naïve, and trusting or whether it was my old traumas causing me to be suspicious. Everything that had seemed simple when I made the decision to trust him was once again up in the air. The only thing I knew was that my intuition was telling me something was off.

At the time I was taking part in a training on embodied sovereignty with a company called Togetherness. In the course, we learnt to speak up, express ourselves and set boundaries. I understood what the lesson was. My next step was to speak my embodied truth – honestly and fearlessly – without worrying about how it would be received or censoring my feelings.

Speaking up and telling him how I felt was one of the scariest things I'd ever done. It went against every dating strategy that said women should play hard to get and be easy-going. It also was the opposite of the hardened dating persona that kept my emotions buried.

The question rose within me: *what would it be like to speak my truth?*

What even was my truth? I trembled as I realised how divorced from my voice I had been – how I had suppressed it, compromised it, buried it, ignored it. Why was I so afraid to speak out? I wanted to roar loudly in my power and not care anymore who heard me. But still I felt afraid.

One evening, we spoke on the phone, and I planned to tell him how I was feeling. As we casually chatted about our days, I was tempted to brush the issue under the carpet like I'd done so many times in the past with others. To keep quiet, swallow down my suspicions and play the role of the happy 'light and breezy' good girl who never expresses anything negative that could jeopardise her relationship.

But I knew I didn't want a man who wasn't totally invested in me. For once, I was willing to put my own needs first – even if it meant scaring him away. With a trembling voice, I told him that my past meant that

I experienced fear of abandonment. Being careful not to blame him, I explained that I was feeling triggered.

It was deeply uncomfortable for me to own my attachment issues and neediness. I hoped he would offer his reassurance, understanding and support, but instead he became angry. He twisted what had happened, accusing me of being needy and misinterpreting his actions. As far as he was concerned this was my stuff and I had to deal with it alone, not put it on him.

My heart sank at his reaction. It was true that these were my wounds and I continued to do my own ongoing healing work, but at the same time I desired a partner who was sensitive to my needs. I wanted a man who could show me he was there for me and help me feel safe to open up to him. I was sad to see this was not the case.

Although I wanted to be trusting and open my heart, I also didn't want to settle or accept less than I deserved. I had learnt to love myself too much to ignore red flags or put up with sub-par treatment. By speaking up, everything became crystal clear. I may have ended the relationship, but I had finally found my voice.

I wanted my needs to be met. I wanted to be understood. I wanted to be loved. I wanted to be fought for. I wanted to be valued. I wanted to be prioritised. I wanted to be supported. I wanted a man who could hold all of me – even the sad, damaged, ugly parts and not flinch. I wanted the man that I'd envisioned in the gong bath who would love the broken parts of me. Now I knew for sure that this man wasn't him. I chose myself.

## THE PATH OF DESIRE

After breaking up with my OM lover everything in my life began to shift. Although the relationship was short-lived, it taught me a lot about my fears around men. Instead of feeling low that it had ended, I felt empowered. For once I'd been true to myself and expressed my needs.

I was still having OM coaching and the philosophy stretched beyond the meditation practice to a whole lifestyle with a big emphasis on taking responsibility for your own experience and being led by desire. This was a new idea for me. Although I followed my joy in life, there were still ways I denied myself and sexuality was a major one of these.

Desire had been an enemy I'd battled against. It often seemed to get me into trouble. In my 20s I had to declare myself bankrupt after running up thousands of pounds of credit card debt that I couldn't afford to pay back on my meagre salary as a local newspaper reporter. I felt ashamed that I'd overspent so much to have nice things and enjoy a comfortable lifestyle instead of living within my means.

My desire for chocolate, sweet things and carbs had also been a cause of shame. As a young girl, I picked up the message that I needed to be thin to be love-able, which started a lifetime of yoyo dieting and feeling guilty about eating. How often have you heard someone call eating food they enjoy being 'naughty'?

I'd also experienced strong longings for men who treated me badly or were not good for me such as my supposed twin flame, the divorcé, and the OM trainer. How could I trust my desire when it so often led me to pain?

After my divorce, I'd spent around three years being celibate because I didn't feel that men could give me the emotional support and commitment I wanted. There's nothing wrong with being celibate or having boundaries, but sometimes it took almost superhuman feats of willpower.

Why didn't I allow myself to have the intimacy I craved? The honest answer was fear. Fear of getting hurt, being rejected, being seen as 'too easy'. But the truth is that coming from a place of fear will never get you the results you want.

When we follow our desires, we have a lot to lose because it's something we really care about. No wonder so many women prefer to ignore the call of what they really want or substitute compensatory desires for the real thing (like eating chocolate when what you really want is connection).

My OM trainer encouraged me to come from another perspective – what did my body want? In those times of celibacy, I had often felt ridiculously frustrated and longed to be touched. It was a case of my body and mind telling me different things. OM was all about getting out of the mind.

I had always viewed casual sex as something slightly degrading in which men used women. Now I opened my eyes and saw it as a way that I could get my own needs met. With this change of perspective, it felt like a whole world of possibility and freedom opened to me. Like a kid with a new toy, I was eager to try out my newfound power.

I contacted an ex who had reached out to me many times since we broke up three years earlier. He lived nearby and I knew he'd be available. This felt both taboo and thrilling, as I'd never behaved in this way before.

I sent him a message saying: "Hi, how are you?"

He instantly replied: "Hi, do you want to meet up?"

Within a couple of texts, a date and time was set for him to visit me. I was shocked how easy it had been.

For the next few days until our date, I was in a state of anticipation. What would it be like to see him again after so many years? Would there still be chemistry between us? Would I really be able to be intimate with him without getting emotionally attached?

When the night finally came, I drank some wine to ease my nerves. We talked for a while, and I was surprised to see how easily the rapport between us returned. He told me that he had missed me and thought about me a lot. That night he ended up staying and was only too happy to fulfil my desires.

The next day I had mixed feelings. After he left, I felt a familiar sense of abandonment as my trauma and anxious attachment reared its head. Even though I knew this wasn't someone I wanted a relationship with, I still wanted him to want me, and I watched my phone for a text. Feelings of being used and rejected started to emerge.

Luckily, I was prepared for this. I had arranged to speak to a friend that day and to have a call with my OM coach. Both encouraged me to see that my mission had been successful – I had given myself the satisfaction of doing what I wanted without fear. Now I had to stay focused on my own needs, rather than getting sucked into the old negative stories of pain and lack. The only question I needed to ask myself was what desire to fulfil next.

A few days later, my ex texted me to ask if we could see each other again. I felt empowered. For once it felt like it wasn't about the man's satisfaction. Suddenly it was all about me.

## TAKING A CHANCE ON LOVE

What would happen if you went after your desires? It was this question that led me in the direction of love. Deep down, I knew what I wanted: the Swedish guy

I'd dated briefly was still in my heart and mind, although six months had passed since I'd last seen him.

I'd felt I had to get on with my life, so I had followed my bliss in other ways – long baths, walks in nature, yoga, dancing and reading. I focused on work, dated other guys and tried to move on. In my heart, I knew he was the one I desired, but I didn't believe I could have him.

I hadn't reached out to him for several reasons. One was that I believed it was the man's job to be the pursuer and a woman's job to passively receive attention – a belief I had been socially conditioned into and held onto like the Gospel, despite the fact it had not brought me great results.

Secondly, I was terrified of rejection. We'd been out of contact for the six months since we broke up, so I had no idea if he was single or even still living in London. But, most of all, I had no idea if he even wanted to hear from me or would respond. After all, doesn't society tell us that it's best to move on after the end of a relationship?

These reasons had kept me apart from him, hoping that he would be the one to reach out first, but in OM they teach you to always follow your desires, even though the path of desire is not always easy. My coach encouraged me, saying that if I felt the pull in that direction there must be something unresolved that I needed to explore.

It was surprising to be encouraged to contact a man, after a lifetime of books, coaches and recovery groups that had encouraged me to do exactly the opposite. I viewed contacting a man as similar to eating a big cupcake or having a spending spree – a temptation that I would live to regret if I gave into it. But this belief hadn't brought me the love I longed for. Maybe it was time to try something different.

My heart was beating fast, and I felt a surge of adrenaline as I typed a text asking him if he'd like to talk and pressed send. I had no idea what his reply would be, but my teacher in the embodied sovereignty course had told me that when you fire arrows in the direction of what you want, it's only your responsibility to fire the arrow, not to control where it lands.

I had fired an enormous arrow towards my desire, and I hoped it would hit the target. But if it didn't, at least I knew that I had tried to create the life of my dreams.

Shaking with nerves, I arranged to go on a walk with a friend to stop myself watching my phone, but I didn't have to wait for long.

The words flashed up on the screen: "Tammy! Yes, I'm totally up for it."

I breathed a big sigh of relief.

## HOW TO GET WHAT YOU WANT

The rule is simple: ask for what you want. There is no need to compromise, to negotiate, to go into your head. There are so many ways that we will try to avoid asking for our desires and follow the path of fear instead.

When you desire arises, notice it and speak it. If you don't, it will come back to bite you. The ability to trust and react to our impulse is healthy and life-affirming. Be deeply loyal to what you believe is most true. Just work out what you want and then ask for it.

This is simple but has been radical and life-changing for me. Learn to trust yourself and let desire guide you.

# EMBODIMENT: ASK FOR
# WHAT YOU WANT

Ask someone for something you desire today. It could be a cup of coffee, a back rub, a lift somewhere, a hug. Ask clearly, cleanly and without any manipulation.

See what kind of feelings arise for you and record them in your journal. Does it make you feel needy, vulnerable, selfish, guilty? Pay attention to the social conditioning that has made you feel like there is something wrong with expressing what you want.

If they say no, ask them again or ask for something else you want. If they say yes, then truly enjoy and congratulate yourself on your success.

Stay true to your desires and keep asking. By firing arrows in the direction of what you want, you'll get closer to living your ideal life. The arrows might not always hit their target but firing them is the important part. You are moving in the direction of your desire.

#TotallyLoveable @mindfuldivas

# CHAPTER EIGHT

# MINDFUL DATING AND RELATIONSHIP SKILLS

"Full attention is the deepest expression of love."
– Jiddu Krishnamurti

I've left this chapter until last because I truly believe that having the love and relationship of your dreams is an inside job. Please don't skip forward to this chapter, it's important that you do the personal healing work first.

As you learn to love yourself, honour yourself and be more in touch with your needs, you will automatically begin to attract healthier people into your life. However, there are some mindful attitudes towards dating and relationships that you can bear in mind to help you with this journey.

## HEALING WITHIN YOUR RELATIONSHIP

So, what happens once you've manifested your partner and you're in a relationship? As wonderful as being in a partnership is, it's also the place where our wounds can often become most apparent. In some ways, the work of healing is only just beginning.

Even as I was writing this book, new triggers came up for me that showed me places I still needed to work on. In some ways, it felt like a gift reminding me what I needed to write about in this book. No matter how healed I think I am, life always has a way of showing me where I still have wounds.

My personal triggers are anything that makes me feel like I'm being abandoned. Any sign of coldness or withdrawal from a partner and I feel panic rising in me. This is typical of an anxious attachment style. Attachment theory focuses on the emotional bonds between people. British psychologist John Bowlby came up with the idea that the bonds formed with our caregivers in childhood has an impact on how we relate to others in adulthood – particularly in our close relationships.

This theory was later expanded on by psychologist Mary Ainsworth who described three major attachment styles: secure, anxious, and avoidant. If a child knows that a caregiver is stable and available to meet their needs, they will form a secure attachment. If the child is unsure about the availability of their caregiver, they may respond by either withdrawing from them (avoidant) or by trying to re-establish connection (anxious). There is also a fourth type, called disorganised attachment, which exhibits a mixture of avoidant and anxious behaviours.

I relate to being an anxious attachment type and have often experienced worry about how my partners feel about me. At times I've found myself getting into a fight/flight/freeze mode over the most trivial of things. In the early days of my current relationship, I panicked because my partner wanted to cancel a plan we'd made to meet for dinner. This made me feel unloved, neglected and fearful that he'd lost his attraction for me and wanted to end the relationship.

I'd like to say that in that moment I used all my mindfulness skills, but sadly my nervous system became too activated. I began to try out 'protest behaviours', which are ways in which a person with an anxious attachment style tries to provoke a reaction to re-establish communication. I overreacted so much that I was suggesting we end our relationship or take a break. The more my partner stayed calm and reasonable, the more I felt he didn't care and tried to provoke him. The call ended with us deciding to take a few days' break from our usual bedtime calls. The next morning, I woke up with a knot of fear in my stomach, terrified that I'd sabotaged our relationship and we were about to break up. It took me a couple of phone calls chatting through the situation with good friends to feel better. It also helped that he sent me sweet texts throughout the day saying that he wanted to hug me.

The heartbreak I caused myself through this situation simply wasn't worth it. After years of practicing the healing and mindfulness practices outlined in this book, I'd thought that I was done with anxiety and had adopted a secure attachment type. Unfortunately, this was not the case when things didn't go my way. I knew that I needed to really examine myself and prevent these behaviours from happening again that could damage my relationship.

After the argument with my boyfriend over the cancelled date night, I went into panic mode for days. I was worried that now he'd seen an insecure side of me that he wouldn't want to be with me anymore.

When we finally met up, I found out that the whole struggle had been going on in my own head and he wasn't upset with me at all. He saw it all as a storm in a teacup and was confused why I thought such a small incident might threaten our relationship.

The moral of this story is to believe that things will turn out OK. Trust in the benevolence of your partner and of the Universe. Surrendering and trusting that things are going to work out for you is the best thing you can do for yourself and subsequently for your relationship. Choose to respond with calmness to the choppy waves of life and always interpret things in the most positive light possible.

# EMBODIMENT: WHAT'S YOUR ATTACHMENT STYLE?

There are many quizzes you can find online to help you find out what your attachment style is. Make a note of your attachment style and notice how this has played out in your life. It's said that most single people tend to have anxious or avoidant attachment styles, as secure people tend to settle down with other secure people.

If you're anxious or avoidant, think about strategies that can help you to calm your anxiety when in a relationship. You may find yourself either wanting to ask for reassurance (anxious attachment) or push your partner away (avoidant attachment). Instead of indulging these habitual behaviours, try making a list of ways that you can self-soothe. For example:

- Have a bath.

- Chat to a good friend.

- Do yoga.

- Breathing exercises.

- Journaling.

- Dancing.

- Cry and express feelings.

- Spend time in nature.

These are examples of some of things that help me but come up with whatever works for you. Once you have this list, you can refer to it in the moment when you need to look after yourself.

Any time you manage to notice your anxiety spiralling out of control and don't act on it, make sure to recognise and praise yourself for your progress. This is not easy – you're literally rewiring your neural pathways and body. Show yourself some love and appreciation for caring for yourself so well.

#TotallyLoveable @mindfuldivas

# DEALING WITH JEALOUSY

I've always suffered from jealousy in relationships, probably because of my anxious attachment style. Unfortunately, this jealousy has extended to not only when I believe a partner is doing something wrong but also to feeling jealous of their past relationships.

It's embarrassing to say, but when I'm into a man, a part of me wants to be the only one he's ever loved and the one he loves above all others. You're probably rolling your eyes right now and I know these thoughts are completely irrational. Obviously, I don't really want a man who has no prior experience and never dated someone else before because that wouldn't be very attractive. Yet the thought of some-one I love with someone else tears me apart. This has caused me a lot of pain coupled with shame for feeling this way.

When I entered my current relationship, the green-eyed monster started to rear its head again and I was tormented by the idea of my ex with his last girlfriend and other women he'd had relationships with. One day I saw a photo on his phone of him with his ex and started to torment myself that he was happier with her, that she was prettier than me, that he must have loved her more, etc.

Although I was able to use the mindfulness techniques mentioned in this book to help me when these thoughts and feelings came up, I also felt that I needed to work specifically on my jealousy as it had accompanied me for so many years. I wanted to get to the root of where these painful feelings were coming from as I felt that they were not the truest expression of myself.

I began studying the subject of jealousy and what I learnt is that it is a composite emotion. In other words, it is made up of lots of other emotions. What I found helpful was to break those emotions down into smaller pieces to work out exactly what they are made of.

## EMBODIMENT: EXAMINE YOUR JEALOUSY

Think back to the last time you experienced jealousy in your relationship and write it down. Now imagine if the word jealousy didn't exist and try and describe your experience as closely as you can, breaking it down into all the different emotions. Go into as much detail as possible about both your bodily sensations and your thoughts.

For example:

Situation: When I saw him speaking to another woman at a party…

I felt my stomach churning.

I started to feel sick.

I thought she was pretty and that he would be attracted to her.

I felt fear that he would compare her to me and find me lacking.

I wanted him to give his time and attention to me instead of to her.

Etc.

For the next part of this exercise, you examine the underlying beliefs which are driving your jealousy.

For example:

Other women are a threat.

My partner finds other women more attractive than me.

I am not good enough to keep my partner.

If I'm compared to other women, I will be found lacking.

You will find that many of these beliefs stem back to how you feel about yourself, rather than anybody else's behaviour. This is great news because it means that you have the power to change them. After all, you are the only person in life you have any control over.

Rather than jealousy, we could start to describe that composite of emotions as being distress. When I looked very closely at what I was experiencing, I realised that it was a mixture of fear that I would lose someone, combined with feeling that the person I was jealous of was better than me somehow. For example, when I saw photos of his ex on my boyfriend's phone, I was thrown back to my childhood wounds and insecurities.

As you can see, the underlying feelings were really based on my belief that I wasn't good enough. Despite recognising this as being an old story, my nervous system was activated, and I began to feel distressed.

Rather than questioning my boyfriend about his relationship with his ex, what I really needed to do was work on myself, reaffirming my own worth, attractiveness and value. Also it helped to reflect on the value that I bring to my partner's life and the good things about our relationship.

Ultimately you need to realise that you're *Totally Loveable* no matter what. Even if your relationship with your partner was to end, it wouldn't be a reflection on your worth or loveability.

The truth is that our partners can find other people attractive, will have had intimate connections with others in the past and may have other close relationships which are valuable to them

It really helps to see this as a positive thing and feel joy for your partner for having experienced beautiful times and memories and having the ability to create bonds with others. In a way, it makes the relationship you have with your partner even more special because they are choosing to spend their time with you. In the polyamory community, this emotion is known as 'compersion' and it is something which can be cultivated.

In the early days of my current relationship, I sometimes got upset if my partner didn't want to spend time with me when I wanted to spend time with him or had another priority that made me feel neglected. At those times, I reminded myself that he doesn't owe me anything and isn't obligated to me – nor would I want him to be.

We come together every day freely by choice – not out of duty. That makes every time he chooses to be with me and spend the precious moments of his life with me more special. Likewise, I am choosing to spend my precious life with him.

#TotallyLoveable @mindfuldivas

## HEALTHY BOUNDARIES

Until quite historically recently, women didn't have any choice about who they married. These things were determined by their families for economic reasons. I feel that this wound plays into our current time, meaning that many women struggle to speak up in their dating lives. This is all part of being the 'good girl' that we are socially conditioned into.

Even if you don't resonate with the good girl archetype, you may still find there are times when you don't speak up for yourself. These patterns are so deeply ingrained that they are often unconscious and difficult to detect. There are two very key communication skills – learning to ask for what you want (which I discussed in the previous chapter) and learning to say no to what you don't want. Without these dual abilities, you will feel frustrated and unheard.

Do you often find yourself saying 'yes' to things that you don't want to do because you fear upsetting or disappointing others? Sometimes women are too nice, constantly putting themselves last, and feeling too afraid to stand up for themselves or speak their truth.

Are you scared that people won't like you if you say no to them? This can lead to over-committing, exhausting yourself and feeling resentful. All these behaviours will trickle into your romantic and sexual relationships.

In the course I took on embodied sovereignty, the training started with saying the phrase: "I am Tammy, I am real and I am allowed to ask for what I want."

Maybe this is an affirmation you would like to adapt for yourself.

## CLEARING THE THROAT CHAKRA

The throat chakra or *Vishuddha* is the centre associated with communication, expression and speaking your truth. When it is blocked or unbalanced, it can have an impact on your ability to speak clearly and honestly. These are important skills for good relationships, not only with romantic partners but with anyone in your life.

Signs the throat chakra is out of balance include thyroid issues, sore throat, gum disease and other issues in the throat and mouth area.

I was diagnosed with an underactive thyroid in my early thirties and prescribed the hormone replacement medication Thyroxine. This is a common health issue for women after childbirth. However, I believe that it was also related to my inability to express myself.

At the time, I was in a marriage in which my voice wasn't welcomed. My husband even told me that he didn't care about anything I had to say. It was when he said this to me in an argument one day that finally prompted me to realise that relationship was over, but unfortunately it took me many years of being silenced to come to that conclusion.

When I look back, I feel saddened and shocked that I thought it was acceptable to live under those conditions. I remember feeling this strong sensation of being repressed, stifled and pent-up inside. This was not only in my relationship with my husband, it affected all areas of my life, including friendships and work.

As our outer world reflects the inner world, I found myself in friendships with people with very different values to me and being bullied in the workplace. I experienced feelings of helplessness, being stuck and not being listened to or cared about. Reflecting on this really helps me realise how far I have come since those days.

Another symptom of a blocked throat chakra is poor communication. Because I felt unable to speak out for myself honestly and openly, my self-expression came out in other ways. I would make passive aggressive comments at friends rather than communicate clearly, sulk around my husband or get into angry shouting matches. When we would argue, I would physically feel a sense of constriction around my throat as if I was being strangled. I'm even experiencing that sensation as I write this, just through recalling it.

I'm so glad that I'm able to speak out for myself much more these days. It's not always easy and like anything it's an ongoing process, but the more I practise, the more natural it becomes.

One thing that has really helped me is screaming out loud. Before lockdown I attended the women's full moon 5Rhythms dance every month. It's an amazing sight to see a room of women writhing and moving together uninhibited by the presence of men. What is interesting is that without the presence of male eyes, women can be sexier than ever without fear. There is an energy of total abandoned freedom.

My first thought when I walked into the high-ceilinged church hall where the dance was held was: 'This is a room of witches and Goddesses'.

The part which I want to mention right now is a moment in the dance every night when someone screams, and others join in. This isn't initiated by the teacher and seems to be something which occurs spontaneously. At my first full moon dance, I was shocked and a little inhibited, as this was not something I had experienced at other 5Rhythms events. It was the first time I had ever been in a room full of women screaming and it was a primal sound full of passion and pain.

That first time I was too shy to join in with the scream, although a part of me wanted to. As the months went on, I still couldn't let go enough to join in when the screaming inevitably happened, but I began to experiment with allowing myself to make sounds during the dance whether they be grunts, groans, whispers, loud breathing, or anything else that wanted to come through me.

One month, as I danced under the full moon, a scream omitted from my body. The sisters around me joined me and the room echoed with our cries. It had been me who started the scream this time and it was a freeing feeling of releasing so much repressed emotion and energy that was held in my throat and body. Remembering that moment gives me chills even now.

If you have somewhere you can scream, then I recommend it. Unfortunately, in our society, there is not much opportunity to really let go in this way. Maybe you can scream into a pillow or somewhere remote in nature. If this isn't available to you right now, here are some other ways to unblock the throat chakra.

# EMBODIMENT: THROAT CHAKRA ACTIVATION

The energy of the throat chakra welcomes clear communication, self-expression, and mindful listening. Blue is the colour of the throat chakra and imagining a swirling ball of colour there or placing a blue crystal such as amazonite, turquoise, aquamarine or lapis lazuli can help to clear and purify it.

The Hindu mantra for throat chakra is 'ham', which means 'I am she/he/that' in Sanskrit. You can repeat this mantra or look on YouTube for videos which you can chant along with.

Doing neck stretches, wearing blue clothes, eating blueberries and singing can all also heal your throat chakra. Repeating affirmations such as 'I communicate with ease' or 'I always speak my truth' can also help.

#TotallyLoveable @mindfuldivas

# TIME TO YOURSELF

It was only after getting into my current relationship that I realised how much I'd grown to love myself. During my single days, I'd got used to spending my evenings reading, listening to audiobooks, and journaling. Now there suddenly seemed to be much less time for nurturing this important relationship with myself.

When I was single, a part of me had felt that time alone was a poor substitute for being with a partner, but now I saw that this quality time with myself was just as important as time for romance. I'd enjoyed those cosy evenings alone in bed with my notepads and books spread out in front of me. Nothing had ever been missing.

In a committed relationship, it can be easy to start neglecting the things you did when you were single. It's natural to have a honeymoon period when all you want to do is be together every minute of the day, but in the long run it's important to have time to yourself.

This keeps your relationship fresh and interesting and gives you new topics to talk about. In a healthy relationship, you can grow both together and as individuals.

Make sure that you keep up the things that make you the amazing person that you are. For me those things are 5Rhythms, visiting art galleries, creative writing, learning about tantra, Yin yoga, running my women's circle and pampering myself with spa treatments.

## EMBODIMENT: WHAT MAKES YOU UNIQUE?

Write down a list of ways that you want to spend time with yourself. Really think about these specific activities that you enjoy by yourself, rather than as a couple.

These could include things your partner doesn't enjoy. For example, my partner hates cheesy romantic comedies, whereas I love them. I make time to watch them alone, rather than missing out on this indulgent pleasure. Other things that I enjoy doing without my partner include going on retreats, watching the ballet and practicing yoga.

Make a commitment to yourself to make time in your life for the activities that light you up, even when you get busy with your relationship. Schedule dates in your diary or calendar and make sure that you stick to them. Not only will it make you feel better about yourself, but it will keep your relationship vibrant too.

#TotallyLoveable @mindfuldivas

## MINDFUL ATTENTION

Nothing feels better than having somebody's full attention on us. In this time of smartphone addiction, it's actually very rare that anybody really listens to what we say. Be honest, how many times has your mind wandered while someone was speaking to you?

Try putting your full attention on your partner when they speak. Really listen to them closely, watch their lips moving and engage with what they're saying. Look directly at them and nod your head to show them that you care about what they say.

Research by the psychologist John Gottman showed that the extent to which couples responded positively to each other was the biggest indicator of whether they would stay together long-term. In a study of 130 newlywed couples, those who showed interest and support when the other tried to connect with them 87% of the time were more likely to be together six years later, whereas those who only responded positively 33% of the time were more likely to be divorced within six years.

The research also found that showing contempt for a partner was the number one thing that tore relationships apart. It may seem obvious, but simple kindness and attention can do wonders for your relationship.

The following tantric communication games can help increase the connection with your partner and keep the spark alive in a long-term relationship.

## EMBODIMENT: CONNECTION GAMES

### THE THREE MINUTE GAME

The three-minute game was devised by Betty Martin as part of her Wheel of Consent model. Each partner takes a turn at being one of the four quadrants – either taking, receiving, giving or allowing.

To play the game, one partner asks the other: "How would you like to touch me for three minutes?"

The person feels into their body and requests what they would like, then the other partner decides if they are willing to do that for three minutes. If they are not willing, their partner can suggest another way they'd like to be touched. This can be any kind of touch – it doesn't have to be anything overtly sexual or sensual.

Once the time is up, the first partner asks: "How would you like to touch me for three minutes?"

The partner then decides how they would like to touch the other one. If the partner agrees then they carry out the touch for three minutes. This is not for the other's pleasure but for their own, so in this instance the partner doing the touching is 'taking' and the other partner is 'allowing'.

Once the three minutes is over, swap over and repeat the exercise the other way around.

## DESIRES, FEARS, GRATITUDES

In this connection exercise one partner asks the other a series of questions several times. The questions are:

What do you desire?

What do you fear?

What do you love about me?

You can ask each question around five or six times and each time you receive an answer ask the question again. Then move onto the next question.

Once all three questions have been asked, swap over roles so that the other partner asks the questions.

#TotallyLoveable @mindfuldivas

## KEEP YOUR HEART OPEN

Being vulnerable in dating is difficult but in a long-term relationship the stakes are even higher. Each time my relationship with my partner deepens or I reveal another layer of myself, new fears can come up. A part of my heart always wants to close and protect myself.

Recently, I missed an important personal deadline, which I was ashamed of. I didn't want to tell my partner about it because I felt he might judge me, and I didn't want him to see what I perceived as my failing. My ego wanted him to see me as this person who was always mindful and had everything together.

Eventually, when I confided in him, he was very supportive and pointed out to me all the stresses I'd been dealing with at the time that had contributed to me missing the deadline. His kindness made me feel accepted for who I was, however imperfectly I showed up. Yet again, I was reminded that I don't need to be perfect to be loved.

This goes both ways, and we must acknowledge that our partners are not perfect either. They will make mistakes; do things we don't understand and even do things we don't agree with or that hurt us. In these situations, it helps to accept all of them as they are. Can you show up open and available for the fullness of your life together and welcome who you are and who your partner is?

It's a beautiful thing to know someone in each moment without an agenda. Real intimacy comes from knowing the fullness of someone and being present with them. Love is allowing each other to be your full selves.

Of course, this never means accepting abuse or behaviour that is unacceptable to you. We can still hold our boundaries while loving another.

# FEAR OF INTIMACY

If you've been single and looking for a relationship for a long time, you may begin to believe that your potential partners have commitment fears. However, have you ever heard the ancient Hermetic phrase, 'As within, so without'?

In other words, your outer world is always reflecting what's going on inside you. If partners with commitment fears constantly come into your reality, you may want to examine your own views about commitment. We can pick up fears from our parents' relationship, our own past relationships, and general social conditioning, which constantly give us messages about relationships being boring or hard work.

Once you're in a long-term relationship, these fears can reveal themselves even more clearly. They may show up as wanting to distance yourself from your partner, picking arguments, finding fault and general feelings of restlessness or dissatisfaction.

It's a cliché, but have you heard before that intimacy stands for 'into-me-see'? It can be scary to let ourselves be truly seen and the more we get to know someone the more naked we are before them.

If you have any deep fears that in some way you are not good enough, loveable, or worthy of commitment, then these will start to emerge again. Partnerships have a wonderful way of shining a light on all our wounds.

Although this may feel unpleasant, see it for what it is – a wonderful chance to see any remaining blocks and deal with them.

## EMBODIMENT: OWN YOUR INTIMACY FEARS

Go to a quiet place and take a few deep breaths to connect with yourself.

Take your journal and complete the sentences below as many times as possible. Don't analyse your answers too closely – write down the first thoughts that come into your head, even if they don't seem to make sense at first. This is a brainstorming exercise to uncover deep unconscious beliefs, so just go for it.

Complete these two sentences several times:

>If I am truly seen I fear that…
>
>If I commit myself to this relationship, I fear that…

For example:

>If I am truly seen I fear that…
>
>My partner will grow bored of me.
>
>He will see that I'm not good enough.
>
>I will be abandoned.
>
>If he rejects me, I'll know it was because of who I really am.
>
>I could get hurt.

If I commit myself to this relationship, I fear that…

>I could get bored.
>
>I will be trapped.
>
>I will never get to be with someone else
>
>My deepest desires won't be fulfilled.
>
>If he leaves me one day I'll be alone and back to square one.

Once you have this list, examine your list of fears. What came up for you?

See if you can replace the things on your list with positive affirmations about intimacy and commitment instead. One easy way to do this is to write the opposite of your fears. Alternatively, write whatever positive statements come to mind.

For example:

> Intimacy is a beautiful way of connecting with another human being.
>
> Intimacy brings us closer.
>
> The more my partner gets to know me, the more he loves me.
>
> The closer we get, the more deeply we fall in love.
>
> My partner sees more and more beautiful things about me every day.
>
> The more I open up, the more loved and adored I am.
>
> Commitment is normal and natural.
>
> I love being committed to my partner and my partner loves being committed to me.
>
> Commitment allows our relationship to grow and thrive.
>
> I find commitment exciting and interesting.

#TotallyLoveable @mindfuldivas

## CONNECTION RITUALS

One way I love keeping the intimacy in my relationship alive is through connection rituals which have become part of our daily routine. These add to a feeling of safety and security.

One of these is 'morning cuddles' – we always cuddle and kiss for around 15 minutes in the morning before getting out of bed. Another is meeting at 3pm to do an afternoon meditation while holding hands.

We also choose joint projects to work on every month. One of our current goals is to learn more about environmentalism, so we watch a documentary about nature, sustainability, or veganism every week.

You can create your own connection rituals based on which activities best fit into your daily routine and can help you and your partner to connect and bond over shared values.

## AN ABUNDANCE OF LOVE

I often notice people talking to their partners in rude and disparaging ways. Sometimes couples seem to be more polite to complete strangers than to the person they've chosen to spend their life with.

Personally, I think it's important to remember that nobody owes you anything. Your partner or the people you date are under no obligation to do anything at all for you. Treat everything as a gift from their heart no matter how small. Appreciate it if your partner makes you a cup of tea, asks how your day was, takes the rubbish out or buys you dinner. Never take these things for granted or feel entitled to them.

My man does little things for me every day like charging my headphones, bringing me coffee in bed or chopping the onions when I'm cooking because they make my eyes water. I thank him profusely and give him a kiss or a hug every time.

The more appreciated your partner feels, the happier they'll be and the more likely to want to please you. Plus, once you start to fully receive and appreciate every little thing as a gift, you'll realise that you're surrounded by an abundance of love.

# A FINAL WORD

"You've seen my descent. Now watch my rising."
– Rumi

Now that you've finished reading this book, I really hope you can see big shifts in your life, especially around how worthy and deserving you feel of love.

Remember that a change in your perception is a wonderful manifestation in itself. Make sure to celebrate any breakthroughs, no matter how big or small. Take a moment also to thank yourself for showing up on this healing journey – that alone is an amazing demonstration of self-love.

I strongly encourage you to stick to your mindfulness practice and return to this book whenever you need encouragement. The embodiment exercises are intended to be carried out on a regular basis. I still meditate, journal and do my inner work every day. I'm constantly growing and evolving and to me this self-care is just as important as eating healthily or brushing my teeth.

Mindfulness has brought me back to the truth of who I am, and I believe and trust it will do the same for you.

I recommend using the *Totally Loveable Journal* to track your progress on this path. The journal is available from Amazon and includes all the embodiment exercises from this book with space to record your thoughts and experiences.

There are also additional free resources to support you on my website at: **www.themindfuldiva.com/book**

I want to end with these words of wisdom that one of my coaches told me:

"Relationships do not always feel good, but they always bring us more consciousness."

Ultimately this journey isn't about anybody else. It's about your personal realisation that you are *Totally Loveable* no matter what.

Tammy x

# RESOURCES

## BOOKS

Sophie Bashford, (2018), *You are a Goddess*, Hay House UK

Brené Brown, (2010), *The Gifts of Imperfection: Let Go of Who You Think You're Supposed To Be and Embrace Who You Are*, Hazelden Publishing

Rhonda Byrne, (2008), *The Secret*, Simon & Schuster UK

Julia Cameron, (1992), *The Artist's Way*, Souvenir Press

Rebecca Campbell, (2015), *Light is the New Black*, Hay House UK

Nicole Daedone, (2011), *Slow Sex: The Art and Craft of the Female Orgasm*, Grand Central Life & Style

Elizabeth Gilbert, (2009), *Eat, Pray, Love*, Bloomsbury Paperbacks

Neville Goddard, (2013), *The Complete Reader*, Audio Enlightenment

Jackson MacKenzie, (2015), *Psychopath Free*, Berkley – US

Clarissa Pinkola Estés, (1996), *Women Who Run with the Wolves*, Ballantine Books Inc.

Regena Thomashauer, (2003), *Mama Gena's School of Womanly Arts*, Simon & Schuster

Melanie Tonia Evans, (2018), *You Can Thrive After Narcissistic Abuse*, Watkins

## USEFUL LINKS

Breathworks - www.breathworks-mindfulness.org.uk
Institute of OM - www.instituteofom.com
London Buddhist Centre - www.londonbuddhistcentre.com
Betty Martin - www.bettymartin.org
Layla Martin - www.laylamartin.com
Taraloka Buddhist Retreat Centre - www.taraloka.org.uk

Togetherness - www.togetherness.com

Rapid Transformational Therapy - www.marisapeer.com

Rape Crisis- www.rapecrisis.org.uk

5Rhythms - www.5rhythms.com

## TAMMY'S RESOURCES

*Totally Loveable* free resources -
www.themindfuldiva.com/book

*Totally Loveable Journal* - Available from Amazon

Work with Tammy through coaching -
www.themindfuldiva.com/coaching

Awakening Women's Circle -
www.themindfuldiva.com/womens-circles

# ACKNOWLEDGEMENTS

I'd like to extend my gratitude to everyone who helped me birth this book into the world. To my friends and family, thank you all for your support. Special thanks to Mel, Joel and Becca for persuading me to leave in all the juicy bits that I wanted to take out! I hope you'll be there to drink some champagne and celebrate with me.

Thank you to Leah for the book design and patiently guiding me through the book creation process. Also, thanks to Jen for the editing and to Hannah for admin support.

I'm lucky enough to have some amazing mentors. Thank you to Ginny for guiding me in my mindfulness practice and to my business coach Emma for helping me believe that anything is possible. Also, I'm very grateful for the support of London Writers' Salon which got me though the writing and editing process.

I'd like to take this opportunity to say a huge thank you to my wonderful readers, followers, women's circle members and all the lovely people who have been part of my mindfulness courses over the years. I've enjoyed working with you all so much and your support has made this book possible.

Finally thank you to the Swedish guy Henrik for making me feel *Totally Loveable* and to my daughters Maisie and Enid who are the true loves of my life.

# ABOUT THE AUTHOR

**Tammy Lovell** is a mindfulness teacher, life coach, women's circle leader and award-winning health journalist. She is a registered teacher with the *British Association of Mindfulness Based Approaches (BAMBA)* and her company *The Mindful Diva* is dedicated to guiding people to overcome stress, anxiety and chronic pain so they can fulfil their purpose in the world.

Tammy started her mindfulness journey back in 2013 when she went through a difficult divorce. After initially turning to alcohol to cope, she went through a personal breakdown which saw her on the verge of losing everything dear to her. At her lowest point she discovered a meditation retreat, which led to a spiritual awakening and a new way of life. After studying mindfulness and coaching, Tammy quit her media job to focus on helping others who are suffering and looking for guidance.

In 2020, Tammy co-founded *Awakening Women's Circle* with a friend as an online offering to help women feeling alone during global coronavirus lockdowns. Tammy now writes and teaches about mindfulness, health and relationships full-time.

She has been featured in publications including *Soul & Spirit*, *The Mail on Sunday*, and *Menopause Life*. When not focused on her business, Tammy spends her time chilling out with her family and pet guinea pigs.

www.themindfuldiva.com
@mindfuldivas